SOUTH-SIDE VIEW OF

SLAVERY;

OR,

THREE MONTHS AT THE SOUTH,

IN 1854.

BY

NEHEMIAH ADAMS, D. D.

NEGRO UNIVERSITIES PRESS
NEW YORK

Originally published in 1854
by T. R. Marvin, Boston

Reprinted 1969 by
Negro Universities Press
A DIVISION OF GREENWOOD PUBLISHING CORP.
NEW YORK

Library of Congress Catalogue Card Number 69-16593

SBN 8371-1531-0

PRINTED IN UNITED STATES OF AMERICA

INTRODUCTORY STATEMENT.

SOME things in the history of this book afford an illustration of the undesirableness of answering a matter before we hear it. A preliminary correspondence of mine with a southern gentleman has brought forth a singular combination of feelings and expressions, all founded on a mistake; which is, that the writer of this book sought to conciliate a slaveholder with the proposition of a compromise between the north and south, by which northern opposition to slavery should be diverted and allayed. A plain statement may remove disagreeable feelings and apprehensions.

Much of this book was written at the south. On completing it at home, the writer wished to fortify himself in certain statements, and therefore wrote letters, with different sets of questions, to different gentlemen at the south, but with no intention to publish their answers. One of these gentlemen was Hon. H. A. Wise, of Virginia. That he, in his way, as the writer well knew, is a representative man on the subject of slavery, none will now dispute. I approached him fairly and honorably. I disclosed my object so far as was necessary to secure his attention, and I gained the purpose for which I wrote; so that on reading his letter in manuscript, and seeing that it confirmed the statements which I had written for my book, I acknowledged the favor in a note of thanks. The letter, read in private, did not offend me, because I saw that the writer was not combating me personally; and I thought of it

(3)

only in one light, — viz., as making it unnecessary for me to correct my manuscript, which was nearly ready for the press. When the correspondence afterward came forth from Mr. W., without my consent, in the Washington (D. C.) Union, his letter had a different bearing. I was placed in a new relation toward him, and was sorry that he compelled me to speak to him as I did in my reply.

And now this book is the development of my wishes and purposes so imperfectly expressed in my private letter to Mr. Wise. The book stands just as it did when I wrote that letter. I am not responsible for any expectations or disappointments with regard to this book occasioned by a letter which I did not write for publication, and never intended as a description of this volume. The book has been finished according to its first design.

As some have held forth Mr. Wise's letter as a true exponent of a slaveholder's spirit, it is due from me to say that, with that letter, I received other communications from southern gentlemen on the same subject. Answers to inquiries, so obliging, so regardful of the supposed difficulty which suggested a question, so generous in affording information, so candid, I have seldom known. Any who wish, may argue from them that the effect of slaveholding upon a gentleman's spirit and manner is eminently happy.

A counterpart to Mr. Wise's letter appeared in the New York Independent of October 12, in an article on my correspondence with Mr. W. If the writer had waited for correct knowledge of the facts in the case, he might have written more discreetly. When I first heard of the piece, the whole of this book was in type.

Watching in a sick room far from home, new affections are awakened toward our fellow-men; sectional feelings are diminished; and every subject, public as well as private, is viewed in connection with our higher and enduring interests and relations. Under such influences many of these pages were written, some of them containing strictures which, in a chastened state of mind, one can make with the consciousness of being actuated only by good motives.

The thought of writing a book on this subject never occurred to me till I had experienced much surprise and pleasure at certain new impressions from slavery at the south. They who think that these impressions were owing to partial views of American slavery will see their mistake. Should I relieve the minds of a few friends on this subject, as mine has been relieved, my labor will not be lost. But it is proper to say, that while preparing these pages, from the beginning to the close, things have come to my knowledge with regard to slavery which took away, at the time, the power to think or speak of it except in the tone of reprobation. Feelings more discriminating and no less just have alternated with these, and the result is here given.

No one can expect to find, nor do I think to give, in this book, a full exposition of the subject of slavery. Yet I trust it will be seen that I have gathered premises broad enough for all the conclusions which I have ventured to draw.

Now, if any friend of mine, who, knowing me, knows that I am no partisan, will intrust himself to my guidance, I will take him with me in this book to the south, and we will together look at the things which happen to meet us, receive the impressions which they may naturally make, and if we differ and part company, we will endeavor to do so with mutual respect and affection.

CONTENTS.

(vii)

viii   CONTENTS.

A
SOUTH-SIDE VIEW OF SLAVERY.

CHAPTER I.

FEELINGS AND EXPECTATIONS ON GOING TO THE SOUTH.

It was well said by Rev. John Newton, of London, that Job and his friends might have continued their dispute to the present time, if they had lived so long, unless God had interposed to settle the controversy.

Good men, conscientiously persuaded of the truth and importance of their respective partial views of a great subject, pleading for God, and therefore convinced, each of them, that the Most High is on his side, cannot yield one to the other without doing violence to their consciences.

Some new development, some providential disclosure, must be made to withdraw their thoughts from the issue which, they insist, is the only one of which the subject is capable ; otherwise, that which was mere contrariety of opinion grows to alienation and strife, of which no one sees the end.

He who proposes to write or speak at the present time on the subject which has so long tried the patience of good men as the subject of slavery has done, is justi-

(7)

fied in asking attention only by the conviction which it
is supposed he feels that he can afford some help.

The writer has lately spent three months at the south
for the health of an invalid. Few professional men at
the north had less connection with the south by ties of
any kind than he, when the providence of God made it
necessary to become for a while a stranger in a strange
land. He was too much absorbed by private circumstances to think of entering at all into a deliberate consideration of any important subject of a public nature;
yet for this very reason, perhaps, the mind was better
prepared to receive dispassionately the impressions which
were to be made upon it. The impressions thus made,
and the reflections which spontaneously arose, the writer
here submits, not as a partisan, but as a Christian; not
as a northerner, but as an American; not as a politician,
but as a lover and friend of the colored race. Having
unexpectedly experienced help and relief in some degree in contemplating the subject, perhaps others may
be assisted by noticing the process through which it was
derived. To give information about slavery, to depict
scenes at the south, to add any thing to the almost num-
berless discussions of the subject, is not the object of
this book.

I will relate the impressions and expectations with
which I went to the south; the manner in which things
appeared to me in connection with slavery in Georgia,
South Carolina, and Virginia; the correction or confirmation of my northern opinions and feelings; the conclusions to which I was led; the way in which our language
and whole manner toward the south have impressed me;
and the duty which it seems to me, as members of the
Union, we at the north owe to the subject of slavery and

to the south, and with the south to the colored race. I shall not draw upon fictitious scenes and feelings, but shall give such statements as I would desire to receive from a friend to whom I should put the question, "What am I to believe? How am I to feel and act?"

In the few instances in which I do not speak from personal observation, I shall quote from men whom, in many places at home and abroad, I have learned to respect very highly for their intellectual, moral, and social qualities — I mean physicians. Associated with all classes at all times, knowing things not generally observed, and being removed by their profession from any extensive connection with slavery as a means of wealth, they have seemed to me unusually qualified to testify on the subject, and their opinions I have found to be eminently just and fair.

Very early in my visit at the south, agreeable impressions were made upon me, which soon began to be interspersed with impressions of a different kind in looking at slavery. The reader will bear this in mind, and not suppose, at any one point in the narrative, that I am giving results not to be qualified by subsequent statements. The feelings awakened by each new disclosure or train of reflection are stated without waiting for any thing which may follow.

JUST before leaving home, several things had prepared me to feel a special interest in going to the south.

The last thing which I did out of doors before leaving Boston was, to sign the remonstrance of the New England clergymen against the extension of slavery into the

contemplated territories of Nebraska and Kansas. I had
assisted in framing that remonstrance. The last thing
which I happened to do late at night before I began my
journey was, to provide something for a freed slave on
his way to Liberia, who was endeavoring to raise several
thousand dollars to redeem his wife and children from
bondage. My conversations relating to this slave and
his family had filled me with new but by no means
strange distress, and the thought of looking slavery in
the face, of seeing the things which had so frequently
disturbed my self-possession, was by no means pleasant.
To the anticipation of all the afflictive sights which I
should behold there was added the old despair of seeing
any way of relieving this fearful evil, while the unavail-
ing desire to find it, excited by the actual sight of wrongs
and woe, I feared would make my residence at the south
painful.

Behind the tables at the hotel in New York, on my
way south, stood a row of black waiters — no unusual
sight to me, indeed ; but with my thoughts of the south
and the slaves, it assumed new interest. I connected
them in my thoughts with the slaves. They seemed
like straggling cinders at no great distance from the
burning house which I was about to see. New sympathy for the slave was excited by their visages. If
these who are free wear such dreary looks as my own
thoughts imparted to them, how fearful must be the
faces of the bondmen ! I felt that I was in the entrance
way to the home of a race who would excite in me only
sorrow.

On board the steamship from New York to Savannah,
white faces took the place of the black complexion which
had become identified with serving men. We belong

to a slave State, was the obvious reason given for this substitution. Free negroes could not be received at the southern port; slaves belonging to the steamer could not be trusted at New York; hence those white servants, whose faces, to an eye which retained the recent impression of shining black skin, looked paler than ever.

We had been three days in a southern steamer, and had sailed by Delaware, Maryland, Virginia, North and South Carolina, and had seen no slave. The sight was yet in reserve; curiosity, sympathy, pity, the whole assemblage of northern fancies and feelings which gather together at the mention of a slave, were "all hands on deck" as we entered Savannah River. Climate now ceased to be the only object of interest connected with the south. There lay the rice plantations; but where were the slaves? Some feeling of dread was mingled with curiosity. Cowper's lines, learned and declaimed so often in boyhood, came to mind : —

"O for a lodge in some vast wilderness," &c.,
"I would not have a slave to till my ground," &c.,

with the poet's enumeration of cruelties and horrors. The anticipation of hearing those groans which three millions of our fellow-countrymen are represented in our Fourth of July orations, and which I had myself in such an oration many years ago represented, as sending up to Heaven day and night, and the clanking of those chains which on such occasions are said to be mingling with John Adams's category of joyful noises forever to usher in the nation's birthday, and the confident expectation of seeing at the landing, or in passing through the market-place, a figure like the common touching vignette of a naked negro on one knee, with manacled hands raised imploringly and saying, " Am I not a man and brother ? " had made the thought of reaching the south increasingly painful.

" So you are going south," said a good friend in Boston. " Well," he continued, " you will, I suppose, have your feelings of humanity strongly appealed to many a time." I felt afraid to trust myself in scenes such as I had heard described; yet, as we came near Savannah, there was a natural impatience to see and feel the direful object of so much anticipation.

Within five miles of Savannah the steamer ran aground, in the early fog of a warm day; and as the tide was ebbing, there seemed to be for the time no relief, except as the agents in the city might learn our situation through their spyglasses, or a passing boat report us. The Florida steamer came alongside, took off some passengers for Florida, and left us with our paddle wheels out of water, and not even a slave to pity and help us, and to be an object of pity, from me at least, in return.

A steam tug returning from the mouth of the river came alongside about noon, and took the passengers and their baggage to the city.

On board this tug I looked for the first time in my life upon a slave. All hands on board were slaves. As the boat labored up the stream, I had leisure to indulge my eyes and thoughts in looking at them. Two, with unquestionable marks of servitude in their whole appearance, were talking together in the stern of the boat, the broad brims of their old black hats flapping in the wind over their faces, hiding partly the glances which they gave me as they noticed my interested looks

at them.   One of them whispered covertly to the other,
and both smiled with a kindly look.   It was a different
look from that which you receive in a prison yard, where
shame and pain steal out in quick, uneasy glances.   I
felt impelled to speak with them, but was not yet sufficiently at home.

In the growth of the human mind, fancy takes the
lead of observation, and through life it is always run-
ning ahead of it.   Who has not been greatly amused,
sometimes provoked, and sometimes, perhaps, been
made an object of mirth, at the preconceived notions
which he had formed of an individual, or place, or coming event?   Who has not sometimes prudently kept his
fancies to himself?   Taking four hundred ministers of
my denomination in Massachusetts, and knowing how
we all converse, and preach, and pray about slavery, and
noticing since my return from the south the questions
which are put, and the remarks which are made upon
the answers, it will be safe to assert that on going south
I had at least the average amount of information and
ignorance with regard to the subject.   Some may affect
to wonder even at the little which has now been disclosed of my secret fancies.   I should have done the
same in the case of another; for the credulity or simplicity of a friend, when expressed or exposed, generally
raises self-satisfied feelings in the most of us.   Our
southern friends, on first witnessing our snow storms,
sleigh rides, and the gathering of our ice crops, are full
as simple as we are in a first visit among them.   We
"suffer fools gladly, seeing" that we ourselves "are wise."
Some intelligent men at the south, who have never seen
Lowell, will speak of our "operatives" in a way to excite quite as much mirth as their northern visitors occa-

sion. We both need forbearance and charity one from the other.

How to say enough of preconceived notions respecting slavery, so as to compare subsequent impressions with them, and yet not enough to give southern friends room to exult and say that we all have false and exaggerated notions about slavery, is somewhat difficult. At the risk of disagreeable imputations, and with a desire to be honest and ingenuous, I will merely add, that there was one thing which I felt sure that I should see on landing, viz., the whole black population cowed down. This best expresses in a word my expectation. "I am a slave," will be indented on the faces, limbs, and actions of the bondmen. Hopeless woe, entreating yet despairing, will frequently greet me. How could it be otherwise, if slavery be such as our books, and sermons, and lectures, and newspaper articles represent? nay, if southern papers themselves, especially their advertisements, are to be relied upon as sources of correct impressions?

CHAPTER II.

ARRIVAL AND FIRST IMPRESSIONS.

THE steam· tug reached the landing, and the slaves were all about us. One thing immediately surprised me; they were all in good humor, and some of them in a broad laugh. The delivery of every trunk from the tug to the wharf was the occasion of some hit, or repartee, and every burden was borne with a jolly word, grimace, or motion. The lifting of one leg in laughing seemed as natural as a Frenchman's shrug. I asked one of them to place a trunk with a lot of baggage; it was done; up went the hand to the hat — "Any thing more, please sir?" What a contrast, I involuntarily said to myself, to that troop at the Albany landing on our Western Railroad! and on those piles of boards, and on the roofs of the sheds, and at the piers, in New York! I began to like these slaves. I began to laugh with them. It was irresistible. Who could have convinced me, an hour before, that slaves could have any other effect upon me than to make me feel sad? One fellow, in all the hurry and bustle of landing us, could not help relating how, in jumping on board, his boot was caught between two planks, and "pulled clean off;" and how "dis ole feller went clean over into de wotter," with a shout, as though it was a merry adventure.

One thing seemed clear; they were not so much

cowed down as I expected. Perhaps, however, they were a fortunate set. I rode away, expecting soon to have some of my disagreeable anticipations verified.

In pursuance of the plan indicated in the beginning, I shall now relate the impressions which were involuntarily made upon me while residing in some of the slave States. As before mentioned, I was making no deliberate investigations, and had no theory to maintain; but the things which daily passed before me led to reflections and conclusions, which will appear, some of them, as we proceed, but more especially in the review. Should these pages meet the eyes of any to whom the things here described are perfectly familiar, they will read them with forbearance, and remember that the writer's object is not to give descriptions, but just to relate those things which led him to certain reflections and conclusions; these conclusions alone, so far as they may be useful, constituting the purpose of the book.

All things being arranged at your resting-place, the first impulse is to see how the land lies, settle certain landmarks, and, above all things, find the post-office.

The city of Savannah abounds in parks, as they are called — squares, fenced in, with trees. Young children and infants were there, with very respectable colored nurses — young women, with bandanna and plaid cambric turbans, and superior in genteel appearance to any similar class, as a whole, in any of our cities. They could not be slaves. Are they slaves? "Certainly," says the friend at your side; "they each belong to some master or mistress."

In behalf of a score of mothers of my acquaintance, and of some fathers, I looked with covetous feelings upon the relation which I saw existed between these nurses and children. These women seemed not to have the air and manner of hirelings in the care and treatment of the children; their conversation with them, the degree of seemingly maternal feeling which was infused into their whole deportment, could not fail to strike a casual observer.

Then these are slaves. Their care of the children, even if it be slave labor, is certainly equal to that which is free.

"But that was a freeman who just passed us?"

"No; he is Mr. W.'s servant, near us."

"He a slave?" Such a rhetorical lifting of the arm, such a line of grace as the hand described in descending easily from the hat to the side, such a glow of good feeling on recognizing neighbor B., with a supplementary act of respect to the stranger with him, were wholly foreign from my notions of a slave. "Where are your real slaves, such as we read of?"

"These are about a fair sample."

"But they seem to me like your best quotations of cotton; where are your 'ord., mid. fair to fair, damaged, and poor'?"

Our fancies with regard to the condition of the slaves proceed from our northern repugnance to slavery, stimulated by many things that we read. The every-day life, the whole picture of society at the south, is not presented to us so frequently — indeed it cannot be, nor can it strike the mind as strongly — as slave auctions and separations of families, fugitives hiding in dismal swamps, and other things which appeal to our sensibilities. Whatever else may be true of slavery, these things, we say, are indisputable; and they furnish materials for the fancy to build into a world of woe.

Without supposing that I had yet seen slavery, it was nevertheless true that a load was lifted from my mind by the first superficial look at the slaves in the city.

It was as though I had been let down by necessity into a cavern which I had peopled with disagreeable sights, and, on reaching bottom, found daylight streaming in, and the place cheerful.

A better-looking, happier, more courteous set of people I had never seen, than those colored men, women, and children whom I met the first few days of my stay in Savannah. It had a singular effect on my spirits. They all seemed glad to see me. I was tempted with some vain feelings, as though they meant to pay me some special respect. It was all the more grateful, because for months sickness and death had covered almost every thing, even the faces of friends at home, with sadness to my eye, and my spirits had drooped. But to be met and accosted with such extremely civil, benevolent looks, to see so many faces break into pleasant smiles in going by, made one feel that he was not alone in the world, even in a land of strangers.

How such unaffected politeness could have been learned under the lash I did not understand. It conflicted with my notions of slavery. I could not have dreamed that these people had been " down trodden," " their very manhood crushed out of them," " the galling yoke of slavery breaking every human feeling, and reducing them to the level of brutes." It was one of the pleasures of taking a walk to be greeted by all my colored friends. I felt that I had taken a whole new race of my fellow-men by the hand. I took care to notice each of them, and get his full smile and salutation; many a time I would gladly have stopped and paid a good price for a certain "good morning," courtesy, and bow; it was worth more than gold; its charm consisted in its being unbought, unconstrained, for I was an entire stranger. Timidity, a feeling of necessity, the leer of obliged deference, I nowhere saw; but the artless, free, and easy manner which burdened spirits never wear. It was difficult to pass the colored people in the streets without a smile awakened by the magnetism of their smiles. Let any one at the north, afflicted with depression of spirits, drop down among these negroes, walk these streets, form a passing acquaintance with some of them, and unless he is a hopeless case, he will find himself in moods of cheerfulness never awakened surely by the countenances of the whites in any strange place. Involuntary servitude did not present itself to my eye or thoughts during the two weeks which I spent in Savannah, except as I read advertisements in the papers of slaves for sale.

How the appearance of the colored people in villages and plantation districts would compare with that of city household servants, was a question which was reserved for future observation.

CHAPTER III.

NEW VIEWS OF THE RELATIONS OF THE SLAVES.

THE gentleman at whose house I was guest commanded the military battalion. The parade day occurred during my visit. Three bands came successively within an hour in the morning to salute him. These bands were composed of slaves, so called; but never did military bands suggest the idea of involuntary servitude less, or feel servitude of any kind for the time less, than these black warriors. They approached with their quickstep tunes, formed in front of the dwelling, faced the street, (a respectful manœuvre, unlike our salutes, which make us all face the music,) performed their salute, and marched off in good style. Their personal appearance was in several instances very striking. One of the bass drummers was a fine specimen of the human frame, his points set off by his tight military dress, while a pair of green periscopic spectacles gave an additional touch to his looks. There was nothing grotesque in their appearance, nothing corresponding to Ethiopic minstrelsy in our northern caricatures; any military company at the north would have feelings of respect for their looks and performances.

Going out with a friend to see the line formed, he asked me to accept a cane for the walk. On declining, I was pressed to take it by the remark that I surely

would if I would read the inscription : " From the live
oak of the frigate Constitution, presented," &c. What
had Georgians to do with that frigate, I said to myself,
the frigate which was the pride and boast of us Massachusetts boys in the war?

The thought of our family of States came over me,
our States like the sea, " its waves many, its waters one,"
each claiming the frigate Constitution as hers, "gallant
Hull " hers, our whole naval renown hers. Cords of
love stronger than death holds us together; when the
attempt to break our Union begins to draw upon these
secret bands, they will be found invincible. Petulant,
angry members of the household will frequently threaten,
like passionate children, to leave the house. Let them
try. They will find secret weaknesses and childlike re-
lentings interfering with their sturdy anger, and tears
will start unbidden in better moments.

As the line was forming on " the Bay," the tender of
a locomotive happened to be drawn along on trucks, between the spectators and the military, on its way to the
railroad station. The name of the engine and tender,
in large letters, on the tender, was NEW HAMP-
SHIRE. My New England feelings arose and glowed
within me. It was weak, perhaps, to feel any thing like
a tear, even of pleasure; but the sudden presentation of
a proud New England name, the momentary commin-
gling there in Georgia of north and south, the kind
blending of Nebraska and Anti-Nebraska in that accidental meeting, the easy, home feeling with which the
New Hampshire took the liberty to pass along in the
midst of the pageant, and many other similar thoughts
and feelings, made me reflect what a death it would be
if our Union should suffer fratricide or suicide.

The commander of the military on this occasion, though still justly claiming to be a young man, led the Georgia detachment of troops to our north-eastern frontier during our trouble respecting the boundary question. Maine and Georgia were the same country to him. Should the north ever need Georgia soldiers to battle against a common foe, the hands of one who has no superior in all that constitutes a Christian lady will, with the old southern patriotism, tie his sash for him as she did on that morning of the parade.

The tender (but let no one play upon the word from the effect of the cumbersome thing on my feelings) being out of the way, the bands wheeled into marching order, and the battalion went to the parade ground to the music of those colored men, affording a northerner some novel and pleasant thoughts. It was one of the last things which I had expected to see — the soldiers of the south following the music made by such men, their step enlivened, their spirits cheered by them. It was good and pleasant to see them in that unity, the proverbial love of music in the colored race being permitted to gratify itself in discoursing martial sounds to their masters.

When I awoke the next morning, I found that a slight frost had touched some of my northernmost fancies about the slaves. I knew that I had much yet to learn; but I had thus far seen things which had never been related to me, and I took into my reckoning terms which I had wholly neglected in trying to work out at home the problem of human happiness at the south.

If it be less romantic, it is more instructive, to see the fire department of a southern city composed of colored men in their company uniforms, parading, and in times of service working, with all the enthusiasm of Philadelphia or Boston firemen. Thus it is given to the colored population of some cities and towns at the south to protect the dwellings and stores of the city against fire — the dwellings and property of men who, as slave owners, are regarded by many at the north with feelings of commiseration, chiefly from being exposed, as we imagine, to the insurrectionary impulses of an oppressed people. To organize that people into a protective force, to give them the largest liberty at times when general consternation and confusion would afford them the best opportunities to execute seditionary and murderous purposes, certainly gave me, as a northerner, occasion to think that whatever is true theoretically, and whatever else may be practically true, with regard to slavery, the relations and feelings between the white and colored people at the south were not wholly as I had imagined them to be. These two instances of confidence and kindness gave me feelings of affection for the blacks and respect for their masters. Not a word had been said to me about slavery ; my eyes taught me that some practical things in the system are wholly different from my anticipations. " I saw it, and received instruction."

CHAPTER IV.

FAVORABLE APPEARANCES IN SOUTHERN SOCIETY AND IN SLAVERY.

WHEN we find ourselves to have been under wrong impressions, and begin to have our notions corrected, our disposition is to reach an opposite extreme, and to see things in a light whose glare is as false as the previous twilight. I resolved to watch my feelings in this respect, and take the true gauge of this subject.

SECTION I. — *Good Order.*

The streets of southern cities and towns immediately struck me as being remarkably quiet in the evening and at night.

" What is the cause of so much quiet ? " I said to a friend.

" Our colored people are mostly at home. After eight o'clock they cannot be abroad without a written pass, which they must show on being challenged, or go to the guard house. The master must pay fifty cents for a release. White policemen in cities, and in towns patrols of white citizens, walk the streets at night."

Here I received my first impression of interference with the personal liberty of the colored people. The white servants, if there be any, the boys, the apprentices, the few Irish, have liberty; the colored men are under restraint.

But though I saw that this was a feature of slavery, I did not conclude that it would be well to dissolve the Union in order to abolish it. Apart from the question of slavery, it was easy to see that to keep such a part of the population out of the streets after a reasonable hour at night, preventing their unrestrained, promiscuous roving, is a great protection to them, as well as to the public peace. In attending evening worship, in visiting at any hour, a written pass is freely given; so that, after all, the bondage is theoretical, but still it is bondage. Is it an illustration, I asked myself, of other things in slavery, which are theoretically usurpations, but practically benevolent?

From the numbers in the streets, though not great, you would not suspect that the blacks are restricted at night; yet I do not remember one instance of rudeness or unsuitable behavior among them in any place. Around the drinking saloons there were white men and boys whose appearance and behavior reminded me of " liberty and pursuit of happiness " in similar places at the north; but there were no colored men there: the slaves are generally free as to street brawls and open drunkenness. I called to mind a place at the north whose streets every evening, and especially on Sabbath evenings, are a nuisance. If that place could enforce a law forbidding certain youths to be in the streets after a certain hour without a pass from their employers, it would do much to raise them to an equality in good manners with their more respectable colored fellow-men at the south. I had occasion to pity some white southerners, as they issued late at night from a drinking-place, in being deprived of the wholesome restraint laid upon the colored population. The moral and religious character of the colored people at the south owes very much to this restraint.

Putting aside for the time all thoughts of slavery, I indulged myself in thinking and feeling, here is strong government. It has a tonic, bracing effect upon one's feelings to be in its atmosphere; and as Charles Lamb tells us not to inquire too narrowly of every mendicant whether the "wife and six young children" are a fiction, but to give, and enjoy it, so there was a temptation to disregard for the time the idea of slavery, and, becoming a mere utilitarian, to think of three millions of our population as being under perfect control, and in this instance indisputably to their benefit.

The first instance in which I saw slaves, men and women, acting in an associated capacity, was in a colored choir. My object in speaking of this will appear in the sequel. Would that some of my musical friends could enjoy the performances of that choir at that church. A tall, stout negro, with an intelligent face, rose to sing, and his choir stood up. He doubled back his little hymn book in one hand, and held the singing book, doubled back also, in the other, both at arm's length. He put one foot in the chair where he had been sitting, as though for greater purchase, and then pitched the tune with marked distinctness, giving all the parts. Off he started with an explosive note that waked up every echo, beginning, as directed, at the third verse, —

"Fools never raise their thoughts so high."

His arms, his bended knee, his whole body, were instinct with feeling. He made, perhaps, three times as many

notes as were written, counting his slurs, and his division
of white-faced notes into the due allowance of pointed
ones, with other embellishments, all so exciting that the
short yellow girl, the principal alto, with round face and
neat attire, standing next to him, feeling the windage of
his motions and the interruption to the movement by
his crotchets and fancies, stopped singing, shook with
an internal laugh, with an occasional heat-lightning be-
trayal of her beautiful white teeth, which she covered
as quick as possible to conceal her mirth.   She showed
wonderful self-control, and finally succeeded in carrying
her part; but at the next singing, she and the other
girls removed to the other side of the pillar, which they
left between themselves and the leader in self-defence.
He was all the time solemn and devout; his wish evidently being fulfilled, that his heart, whatever might be
said of his voice, might " in tune be found."   An elderly
negro with white hair, his head thrown back; an intensely
black man, of towering stature, in a Petersham coat; a
genteel youth with master's plaid cassimere riding jacket;
and a few women, conspired to sing the hymn with an
effect deeply impressive and edifying, however much
some of the features in the performance might tend for
a moment to divert the feelings.   No sooner was the
benediction pronounced than, in keeping with the custom
in some white congregations of interrupting the thoughts
of the retiring audience by boisterous organ playing,
this choir started a select piece : —

"Hark ! the vesper hymn is stealing," &c.

It being not much after twelve at noon, this vesper was
as little appropriate as the organ playing just mentioned,

but was sanctioned by the practice of those whose example the blacks follow for good or ill.

The impression here made upon me, or rather confirmed and illustrated afresh, was, that the slaves, so far as I had seen, were unconscious of any feeling of restraint ; the natural order of life proceeded with them ; they did not act like a driven, overborne people, stealing about with sulky looks, imbruted by abuse, crazed, stupidly melancholic. People habitually miserable could not have conducted the musical service of public worship as they did ; their looks and manner gave agreeable testimony that, in spite of their condition, they had sources of enjoyment and ways of manifesting it which suggested to a spectator no thought of involuntary servitude. My theory was, that they ought to be perpetually unhappy. I tried to persuade myself that they were. Ten thousands of people are miserable on their account, and my wonder was, that the slaves themselves were not continually verifying and warranting all the distress of which they are the occasion. This is one of those northern fancies which ought not to be confessed, if one has much regard to being ridiculed at the south, and mourned over by some at the north.

Though not having as yet gone so far in looking at slavery as Goldsmith's Traveler had wandered in seeking for the best state of society, I was nevertheless reminded, more than once, of the conclusion to which he came on his return to England, —

" In every government, though terrors reign,
Though tyrant kings or tyrant laws restrain,
How small, of all that human hearts endure,
That part which laws or kings can cause or cure ! "

In churches generally, the colored people occupy the galleries, sometimes including that portion which with us is used by the choir, the singers in such cases sitting below. As a preacher and as a hearer, I have had opportunities to witness their appearance in public worship, and in no case have I seen inattention or sleep. With much fixedness of posture, the face frequently resting on the hand, with the elbow on the rail, some standing, all looking at the speaker, they were an example of decorum, and of that demeanor which encourages a public speaker. In an audience in which a large number of colored people were sitting in the gallery opposite the pulpit, it being somewhat dark, I noticed occasional quiet disclosures of white teeth, like fireflies after dark, as feelings of gratification in one and another, at some affecting expression in the sermon, made them smile.

My surprise and pleasure experienced a high tide as I noticed something which I may find it difficult to make some of my readers understand, or believe.

Coming out of church the first Sabbath which I spent in a country village, I saw a group of colored men standing under the trees around the house, waiting for the rest of the people to pass out. I could not be mistaken in my impression from their looks that they were Christian men. Their countenances were intelligent and happy; but the thing to which I allude, and of which these men gave me my first impression, was, the dress of the slaves.

SECTION II. — *The Dress of the Slaves.*

To see slaves with broadcloth suits, well-fitting and nicely-ironed fine shirts, polished boots, gloves, umbrellas for sunshades, the best of hats, their young men with their blue coats and bright buttons, in the latest style, white Marseilles vests, white pantaloons, brooches in their shirt bosoms, gold chains, elegant sticks, and some old men leaning on their ivory and silver-headed staves, as respectable in their attire as any who that day went to the house of God, was more than I was prepared to see. As to that group of them under the trees, had I been unseen, I would have followed my impulse to shake hands with the whole of them, as a vent to my pleasure in seeing slaves with all the bearing of respectable, dignified Christian gentlemen. As it was, I involuntarily lifted my hat to them, which was responded to by them with such smiles, uncovering of the head, and graceful salutations, that, scribe or Pharisee, I felt that I did love such greetings in the market-places from such people.

Then I fell into some reflections upon the philosophy of dress as a powerful means of securing respect, and thought how impossible it must soon become to treat with indignity men who respected themselves, as these men evidently did; nay, rather, how impossible it already was for masters who would so clothe their servants to treat them as cattle. Further acquaintance with that place satisfied me that this inference was right. There is one southern town, at least, where it would be morally as impossible for a good servant to be recklessly sold, or to be violently separated from his family, or to be abused with impunity, as in any town at the north.

On seeing these men in their Sabbath attire, and feeling toward them as their whole appearance compelled me to do, I understood one thing which before was not explained. I had always noticed that southerners seldom used the word *slaves* in private conversation. I supposed that it was conscience that made them change the word, as they had also omitted it in the Constitution of the United States. But I was soon unable to use the word myself in conversation, after seeing them in their Sabbath dress, and as my hearers, and in families; their appearance and condition in so great a proportion making the idea connected with the word *slave* incompatible with the impressions received from them. Let no one draw sweeping conclusions from these remarks, but wait till we have together seen and heard other things, and in the mean time only gather from what has been said that our fancies respecting the colored people at the south, as well as their masters, are not all of them, probably, correct.

But the women, the colored women, in the streets on the Sabbath, put my notions respecting the appearance of the slaves to utter discomfiture. At the north an elegantly-dressed colored woman excites mirth. Every northerner knows that this is painfully true. Gentlemen, ladies, boys, and girls never pass her without a feeling of the ludicrous; a feeling which is followed in some — would it were so in all — by compunction and shame. It was a pleasant paradox to find that where the colored people are not free, they have in many things the most liberty, and among them the liberty to dress handsomely, and be respected in it.

You do not see the tawdriness of color, the superfluity of yellow, the violations of taste in the dress of the colored women at the south to the degree which you observe in some other places. One reason, if not the chief, is, they each have a mistress, a matron, or young lady, to advise and direct them, and to be responsible in the community for their good appearance. They also wear fabrics and millinery which either good taste, or, at least, means superior to theirs, originally selected for the use of their mistresses and white members of the family. It may seem extravagant to some, but the pride we have in the respectable appearance of children is felt by southern mistresses with regard to their servants. A grotesque, ill-fashioned dress on a female servant appearing in public on the Sabbath, would be sure to be a subject of a hint from a neighbor or friend. My previous images of slaves were destroyed by the sight of those women with dresses which would have been creditable to the population of any town at the north. The most surprising sight of all, as an evidence of real refinement and good taste, was, here and there, a simple straw bonnet with a plain white ribbon, and a black silk dress. Such is the ordinary appearance of the women in a country town on the Sabbath, and indeed in the cities Fashion hardly stretches her influence further. Mixed with these specimens of the putting on of apparel are seen, of course, very plain, humble clothing and turbans, and instances of great neglect in dress.

It must be observed that these people, men and women, were country people, many of them plantation hands. The difference between them and city slaves was only superficial.

SECTION III. — *The Children of the Slaves.*

But of all the touching sights of innocence and love appealing to you unconsciously for your best feelings of tenderness and affection, the colored young children have never been surpassed in my experience. Might I choose a class of my fellow-creatures to instruct and love, I should be drawn by my present affection toward them to none more readily than to these children of the slaves; nor should I expect my patience and affection to be more richly rewarded elsewhere. Extremes of disposition and character, of course, exist among them, as among others; but they are naturally as bright, affectionate, and capable as other children, while the ways in which your instructions impress them, the reasonings they excite, the remarks occasioned by them, are certainly peculiar.

Their attachments and sympathies are sometimes very touching. One little face I shall never forget, of a girl about seven years old, who passed us in the street on an errand, with such a peculiarly distressed yet gentle look, that I inquired her name. A lady with me said that she belonged to a white family, in which a son had recently killed a companion in a quarrel, and had fled. The natural anguish of a sister at some direful calamity in a house could not have been more strikingly portrayed than in that sweet little dark face. It had evidently settled there.

Going to meeting one Sabbath morning, a child, about eight years old, tripped along before me, with her hymn book and nicely-folded handkerchief in her hand, the flounces on her white dress very profuse, frilled ankles, light-colored boots, mohair mits, and sunshade, all showing that some fond heart and hand had bestowed great care upon her. Home and children came to mind. I thought of the feelings which that flower of the family perhaps occasioned. Is it the pastor's daughter? Is it the daughter of the lady whose garden I had walked in, but which bears no such plant as this? But my musings

were interrupted by the child, who, on hearing foot-
steps behind, suddenly turned, and showed one of the
blackest faces I ever saw. It was one of the thousands
of intelligent, happy colored children, who on every
Sabbath, in every southern town and city, make a
northern visitor feel that some of his theoretical opinions at home, with regard to the actual condition of
slavery, are much improved by practical views of it.

SECTION IV. — *Labor and Privileges.*

Life on the cotton plantations is, in general, as severe
with the colored people as agricultural life at the north.
I have spent summers upon farms, however, where the
owners and their hands excited my sympathy by toils
to which the slaves on many plantations are strangers.
Every thing depends upon the disposition of the master.
It happened that I saw some of the best specimens, and
heard descriptions of some of the very bad. In the rice
swamps, malaria begets diseases and destroys life ; in the
sugar districts, at certain seasons, the process of manufacture requires labor, night and day, for a considerable
time.   There the different dispositions of the master
affect the comfort of the laborers variously, as in all
other situations.

But in the cotton-growing country, the labor, though
extending in one form and another nearly through the
year, yet taking each day's labor by itself, is no more
toilsome than is performed by a hired field hand at the
north ; still the continuity of labor from February to
the last part of December, with a slight intermission in
midsummer, when the crop is " laid by," the stalks being
matured, and the crop left to ripen, makes plantation
life severe.

Some planters allow their hands a certain portion of
the soil for their own culture, and give them stated times
to work it; some prefer to allow them out of the whole
crop a percentage equal to such a distribution of land;
and some do nothing of the kind; but their hearts are
made of the northern iron and the steel. It is the common law, however, with all who regard public opinion
at the south, to allow their hands certain privileges and
exemptions, such as long rest in the middle of the day,
early dismission from the field at night, a half day occa-
sionally, in addition to holidays, for which the colored
people of all denominations are much indebted to the
Episcopal church, whose festivals they celebrate with
the largest liberty.

They raise poultry, swine, melons; keep bees; catch
fish; peddle brooms, and small articles of cabinet making; and, if they please, lay up the money, or spend it
on their wives and children, or waste it for things hurtful, if there are white traders desperate enough to defy
the laws made for such cases, and which are apt to be
most rigorously executed. Some slaves are owners of
bank and railroad shares. A slave woman, having had
three hundred dollars stolen from her by a white man,
her master was questioned in court as to the probability
of her having had so much money. He said that he not
unfrequently had borrowed fifty and a hundred dollars
of her, and added, that she was always very strict as to
his promised time of payment.

It is but fair, in this and all other cases, to describe
the condition of things as commonly approved and pre-
vailing; and when there are painful exceptions, it is but
just to consider what is the public sentiment with regard
to them. By this rule a visitor is made to feel that

good and kind treatment of the slaves is the common law, subject, of course, to caprices and passions. One will find at the south a high tone of feeling on this subject, and meet with some affecting illustrations of it.

You may see a wagon from a neighboring town in the market-place of a city or large place, filled with honeycombs, melons, mops, husk mats, and other articles of manufacture and produce, and a white man with his colored servant selling them at wholesale or retail. It will interest your feelings, and give you some new impressions of slave owners, to know that these articles are the property of that servant, and that his master, a respectable gentleman, with disinterested kindness, is helping his servant dispose of them, protecting him from imposition, making change for him, with the glow of cheerfulness and good humor such as acts like these impart to the looks and manner of a real gentleman, who always knows how to sustain himself in an equivocal position.

Had that master overworked his servant in the sugar season, or killed him in the field, we might have heard of it at the north; but this little wagon has come and gone for more than a year on the market days, the master and servant chatting side by side, counting their net profits, discussing the state of the markets, inventing new commodities, the master stepping in at the Savings Bank, on the way home, and entering nine or ten dollars more in Joe's pass-book, which already shows several hundred dollars; and all this has not been so much as named on the platform of any society devoted to the welfare of the slaves. True, there are masters, who, as the psalm sung by the colored choir says, "never raise their thoughts so high;" but it is gratifying to know that such things as these characterize the intercourse of masters and servarfts at the south. Nameless are they, in a thousand cases, and noiseless; but the consciousness of them, and of the disposition and feelings which prompt them, it was easy to see, gives to our wholesale denunciations of slavery a character of injustice which grieves and exasperates not a little.

Probably every northerner feels, on seeing the negro cabins, that he could make them apparently more comfortable on almost every plantation. The negroes themselves could do so, if they chose, in very many cases; but the cabins will strike every one disagreeably at first. We err in comparing them with dwellings suited to people of different habits and choice from those of the colored population at the south. A log cabin, plastered with mud, whether at the south or west, seems to a stranger a mean, pitiable place. I was, however, amused with a man in the cars, whom I overheard complaining that in building a house for his own family, in a new settlement, he was obliged to build with joists and boards, as logs were not to be had. The log cabin is cool in summer and warm in winter. An estimable man, who had been a physician and became a planter, built brick cabins for his people. They grew sick in them, and he was obliged to erect log cabins. A great fire, and at the same time thorough ventilation, are essential to their comfort and health. Both of these are obtained together in the cabins better than in framed or brick dwellings.

SECTION V.— *Personal Protection.*

A strong public sentiment protects the person of
the slave against annoyances and injuries. Boys and
men cannot abuse another man's servant. Wrongs to
his person are avenged. It amounts in many cases to
a chivalric feeling, increased by a sense of utter mean-
ness and cowardice in striking or insulting one who cannot return insult for insult and blow for blow. Instances
of this protective feeling greatly interested me. One
was rather singular, indeed ludicrous, and made considerable sport; but it shows how far the feeling can proceed. A slave was brought before a mayor's court for
some altercation in the street; the master privately requested the mayor to spare him from being chastised,
and the mayor was strongly disposed to do so; but the
testimony was too palpably against the servant, and he
was whipped; in consequence of which the master sent
a challenge to the mayor to fight a duel.

A gentleman, whose slave had been struck by a white
mechanic with whom the servant had remonstrated for
not having kept an engagement, went indignantly to the
shop with his man servant to seek explanation and redress, and in avenging him, had his arm stripped of his
clothing by a drawing knife in the hands of the mechanic.

It is sometimes asserted that the killing a negro is
considered a comparatively light offence at the south.
In Georgia it is much safer to kill a white man than a
negro; and if either is done in South Carolina, the law
is exceedingly apt to be put in force. In Georgia I
have witnessed a strong purpose among lawyers to prevent the murderer of a negro from escaping justice.

There can be no doubt that this disposition is on the increase. I was in Columbia, South Carolina, when the Law Court of Appeals pronounced sentence of death on two young white men for the murder of a negro who had driven them from his garden. Murderers of a white man surely could not have been addressed otherwise than thus by the judge.

" You must remember with painful emotions the bloody tragedy of that peaceful Sabbath morning in which you were the principal actors.

" With a deadly weapon in your hand, and a fatal purpose in your hearts, you went to Shadrack Johnson's humble dwelling, and in the presence of his imploring wife and weeping children, committed the foul murder which your wicked hearts had conceived.

" It was in vain that you relied upon the evidence of your companions to excuse or to extenuate your offence. Previous threats, the preparation of a deadly weapon, the intention to commit a trespass upon his property, and the execution of your fatal purpose, authorized the jury to say that you are guilty.

" We are prepared to see levity and indiscretion in youth; but great crimes like this are generally the result of evil passions long indulged, and of temptations unresisted.

" If in the morning of life you have become habitually reckless by frequent transgression, you must have lived without that moral training which impresses virtuous lessons on the youthful heart; without that religious instruction which teaches God's commandment, 'Thou shalt do no murder,' and that if you keep not this law, you shall surely die.

" You may flatter yourselves with the hope of a pardon. I am not authorized to say how far the governor may be induced 'to temper justice with mercy;' but if this last hope shall fail you, you will be left to 'a fate more fearful than the death of the body.' For such an event, and for such a fate, I would admonish you to prepare."

Not long since, two men were convicted of worrying a negro with dogs, and killing him. They were confined in Charleston jail. The people of their own district meditated a rescue; but the governor, without changing the ordinary course of proceeding in such cases, conveyed them, under military guard, to the district where the murder was committed, and they were executed in sight of their neighbors.

There have been mournful cases in which the murderer of a negro has escaped deserved punishment; but it was not because it was a negro that was killed. The murderers of white people have as frequently obtained impunity. The arguments of lawyers at the bar have been quoted to show that the life of a negro at the south is not equivalent to the life of a white person; even if this be correct, we forget that lawyers, in changing sides, sometimes change their minds, and are unwilling to have their previous views quoted as authority.

The laws allow the master great extent in chastising a slave, as a protection to himself and to secure subordination. Here room is given for brutal acts; barbarous modes of inflicting pain, resulting in death, are employed; but it is increasingly the case that vengeance overtakes and punishes such transgressors.

It is well for themselves that the blacks do not have the temptations which the liberty of testifying against the whites would give them. While they are thus restricted by law, for obvious reasons, from giving testimony, their evidence has its just weight with juries, when it is known. Offenders do not escape more frequently at the south, by legal quibbles, imperfect legislation, and the ingenuity of lawyers than in the free States. The whole impression with regard to personal protection extended over the slaves, as compared with personal safety elsewhere, was far different from that which I had been led to expect.

SECTION VI. — *Prevention of Crime.*

Prevention of crime among the lower class of society is one striking feature of slavery. Day and night every one of them is amenable to a master. If ill disposed, he has his own policeman in his owner. Thus three millions of the laboring class of our population are in a condition most favorable to preservation from crimes against society. But the petty larcenies which swell our public records of crime are, many of them, at the south privately punished, and do not enter into the public enumerations of offences.

A prosecuting officer, who had six or eight counties in his district, told me that during eight years of service, he had made out about two thousand bills of indictment, of which not more than twelve were against colored people. It must follow of necessity that a large amount of crime is prevented by the personal relation of the colored man to a white citizen. It would be a benefit to some of our immigrants at the north, and to society, if government could thus prevent or reach disturbances of the peace through masters, overseers, or guardians. But we cannot rival in our police measures the beneficial system of the south in its distributive agencies to prevent burglaries and arson.

A physician, relating his experience in his rides at night, said that in solitary places, the sudden appearance of a white man generally excited some apprehension with regard to personal safety, but the sight of a black man was always cheering, and made him feel safe. Husbands and fathers feel secure on leaving home for several days, even where their houses are surrounded by negro cabins and the dwellings of the whites are much scattered. The reading of this would awaken a smile in many a southerner, for it is far below the truth.

On reaching the Great Pedee River near midnight, on the way to Wilmington, North Carolina, the passengers leave the cars and go down into a rude scow or raft, to be pulled over the stream. It is a dismal place. Small piles of the pitch pine light wood are burning here and there in place of lamps or moonlight; negroes stand within twelve or fifteen feet of each other, holding aloft a blazing knot, the reflection of the blaze on their dark skins giving them a fiery-red look; while twenty or thirty of them are seen each with baggage on his shoulders, transferring it to the boat. It seems just the place for some fearful catastrophe. The locomotive is far above you on piles, looking over like a frightened horse into the gulf; the yellow water is in the swamps on either hand, with its brood of amphibious creatures; you strike your cane, or foot, against a log, and pieces of phosphorescent wood fly about; all is stagnant and deathlike; you are at your wits' end as to any way of escape from the doleful place without help. The few white male passengers, with a large number of women and children, would be very much at the mercy of those brawny slaves, should they be disposed to assert their power; but the patient looks of the negroes, the silent manner in which they perform their work, the care which they take in properly disposing the smaller pieces of baggage so as not to be crushed by trunks, and their whole appearance of cheerfulness, awaken feelings of affection and gratitude instead of alarm or thoughts of danger. There is something in the apparent meekness of slaves in their work at such times that makes one love them greatly and feel an intense desire to protect them from imperious, unfeeling words and treatment. Their natural passions and propensities sometimes get the mastery over them, because they are men; but they are not predisposed to violence and insubordination.

CHAPTER V.

FAVORABLE APPEARANCES IN SOUTHERN SOCIET.
AND IN SLAVERY — Continued.

SECTION VII. — *Absence of Mobs.*

ONE consequence of the disposal of the colored people as to individual control is, the absence of mobs. That fearful element in society, an irresponsible and low class, is not found at the south. Street brawls and conflicts between two races of laboring people, or the ignorant and more excitable portions of different religious denominations, are mostly unknown within the bounds of slavery. Our great source of disturbance at the north, jealousy and collisions between Protestant and Irish Roman Catholic laborers, is obviated there.

When the remains of Mr. Calhoun were brought to Charleston, a gentleman from a free State in the procession said to a southern gentleman, " Where is your underswell?" referring to the motley crowd of men and boys of all nations which gather in most of our large places on public occasions. He was surprised to learn that those respectable, well-dressed, well-behaved colored men and boys on the sidewalks were a substitute for that class of population which he had elsewhere been accustomed to see with repugnant feelings on public occasions.

SECTION VIII. — *Personal Liberty.*

The personal liberty of the slaves is in contrast with the notions which many hold. To trust them far out of sight, many suppose, is unsafe and very unusual. This is soon corrected on seeing such instances as these which came to my knowledge, and which are not remarkable.

A gentleman sent a slave with a horse and buggy to the plantation of a relative a hundred and ten miles distant, to get some of the herb boneset for an invalid daughter under medical treatment. Ralph was a culler of simples, remembered where the herb grew, and was sure that none could be found short of that plantation. He returned in due time with "a smart heap of it."

I saw a slave who had been sent seven hundred miles, to Washington, D. C., with his master's span of horses and carriage, and a considerable amount of gold. This man was once abducted, with others, at Washington, in a well-known case, but voluntarily returned, with the loss of his watch and money, to his master. The feeling of masters is, that they will not keep a servant who is not willing to remain with them. They are suffered to find other masters. If on fleeing they are pursued, it is to recover them as property; but they are almost invariably disposed of.

SECTION IX. — *Absence of popular Delusions.*

There is another striking peculiarity of southern society which is attributable to slavery, and is very interesting to a northerner at the present day. While the colored people are superstitious and excitable, popular delusions and fanaticisms do not prevail among them. That class of society among us in which these things get root has a substitute in the colored population. Spiritual rappings, biology, second-adventism, Mormonism, and the whole spawn of errors which infest us, do not find subjects at the south. There is far more faith in the south, taken as a whole, than with us. Many things which we feel called to preach against here are confined to the boundaries of the free States; yet the white population are readers of books, though not of newspapers, perhaps more generally than we. That vast amount of active but uninstructed mind with us which seizes every new thing, and follows brilliant or specious error, and erects a folly into a doctrine with a sect annexed, and so infuses doubt or contempt of things sacred into many minds, is no element in southern life. This is one reason why there is more faith, less infidelity, at the south, than at the north. The opinions of a lower class on moral and religious subjects have a powerful effect on the classes above them more than is generally acknowledged; and hence we derive an argument in favor of general education, in which moral and religious principles shall have their important place.

CHAPTER VI.

FAVORABLE APPEARANCES IN SOUTHERN SOCIETY
AND IN SLAVERY—Continued.

SECTION X.—*Absence of Pauperism.*

PAUPERISM is prevented by slavery. This idea is absurd, no doubt, in the apprehension of many at the north, who think that slaves are, as a matter of course, paupers. Nothing can be more untrue.

Every slave has an inalienable claim in law upon his owner for support for the whole of life. He can not be thrust into an almshouse, he can not become a vagrant, he can not beg his living, he can not be wholly neglected when he is old and decrepit.

I saw a white-headed negro at the door of his cabin on a gentleman's estate, who had done no work for ten years. He enjoys all the privileges of the plantation, garden, and orchard; is clothed and fed as carefully as though he were useful. On asking him his age, he said he thought he " must be nigh a hundred; " that he was a servant to a gentleman in the army " when Washington fit Cornwallis and took him at Little York."

At a place called Harris's Neck, Georgia, there is a servant who has been confined to his bed with rheumatism thirty years, and no invalid has more reason to be grateful for attention and kindness.

Going into the office of a physician and surgeon, I accidentally saw the leg of a black man which had just been amputated for an ulcer. The patient will be a charge upon his owner for life. An action at law may be brought against one who does not provide a comfortable support for his servants.

Thus the pauper establishments of the free States, the burden and care of immigrants, are almost entirely obviated at the south by the colored population. While we bow in submission to the duty of governing or maintaining certain foreigners, we can not any of us conceal that we have natural preferences and tastes as to the ways of doing good. In laboring for the present and future welfare of immigrants, we are subjected to evils of which we are ashamed to complain, but from which the south is enviably free. To have a neighborhood of a certain description of foreigners about your dwellings; to see a horde of them get possession of a respectable dwelling in a court, and thus force the residents, as they always do, to flee, it being impossible to live with comfort in close connection with them; to have all the senses assailed from their opened doors; to have your Sabbath utterly destroyed, — is not so agreeable as the presence of a respectable colored population, every individual of which is under the responsible oversight of a master or mistress, who restrains and governs him, and has a reputation to maintain in his respectable appearance and comfort, and keeps him from being a burden on the community.

I thought of our eleven thousand paupers who have been received at Deer Island, in Boston harbor, during the short time that it has been appropriated to that purpose, and of our large State workhouses, which we so patiently build for the dregs of the foreign population. This paragraph from the Boston Post is in place here:—

HOUSE OF CORRECTION.—There were yesterday six hundred and fifty-four prisoners in the House of Correction, with the promise of an addition of thirty more before to-morrow. The accommodations are so limited that about one hundred of them are compelled to sleep in one of the workshops, and it is the intention of the master to place a part of them in the chapel. So many are there, that it is difficult to find any thing for a large portion of them to do; and sometimes from eighty to one hundred are idle. When a call is made upon any of the idle ones to do any work out doors, they jump with great alacrity to perform it, being delighted to have an opportunity to breathe the fresh air.

The south is saved from much of this by her colored laboring class. We may say that we prefer even this to slavery without it. They may reply as one of the Sacs and Fox Indians said in his speech at our State-House several years ago to the governor, alluding to our peninsula: "We are glad you have got this island, and hope you are contented with it."

The following case, that came to my knowledge, offers a good illustration of the views which many slaves take of their dependent condition. A colored woman with her children lived in a separate cabin belonging to her master, washing clothes for families in that place. She paid her master a percentage of her earnings, and had laid up more than enough to buy her freedom and that of her children. Why, as she might be made free, does she not use it rather?

She says that if she were to buy her freedom, she would have no one to take care of her for the rest of her life. Now her master is responsible for her support. She has no care about the future. Old age, sickness, poverty, do not trouble her. "I can indúlge myself and children," she says, " in things which otherwise I could not get. If we want new things faster than mistress gets them for us, I can spare money to get them. If I buy my freedom, I cut myself off from the interests of the white folks in me. Now they feel that I belong to them, and people will look to see if they treat me well." Her only trouble is, that her master may die befòre her ; then she will " have to be free."

SECTION XI. — *Wages of Labor.*

One error which I had to correct in my own opinions was with regard to wages of labor. I will illustrate my meaning by relating a case.

A young colored woman is called into a family at the south to do work as a seamstress. Her charge is, perhaps, thirty-seven and a half cents per day.

"Do you have your wages for your own use?" "No; I pay mistress half of what I earn."

Seamstresses in our part of the country, toiling all day, you will naturally think, are not compelled to give one half of their earnings to an owner. This may be your first reflection, accompanied with a feeling of compassion for the poor girl, and with some thoughts, not agreeable, concerning mistresses who take from a child of toil half her day's earnings. You will put this down as one of the accusations to be justly made against slavery.

But, on reflecting further, you may happen to ask yourself, How much does it cost this seamstress for room rent, board, and clothing? The answer will be, nothing. Who provides her with these ? Her mistress.

Perhaps, now, your sympathy may be arrested, and may begin to turn in favor of the mistress. The girl does not earn enough to pay her expenses, yet she has a full support, and lays up money.

Could we make such provision for the army of seamstresses who work for the shops in New York and other large places, making shirts at six or eight cents each, and paying rent and board out of this, we should feel that one heavy burden was lifted from our hearts ; and certainly it would be from theirs. I compared the condition of those colored seamstresses with that of the seamstresses of London so often described and sung. Thomas Hood has caused this inscription to be placed on his monument: " He sung the Song of the Shirt." Had he never seen any seamstresses but those who are American slaves, he would not have had occasion to write that song.

The accusation against slavery of working human beings without wages must be modified, if we give a proper meaning to the term *wages*. A stipulated sum per diem is our common notion of wages. A vast many slaves get wages in a better form than this — in provision for their support for the whole of life, with permission to earn something, and more or less according to the disposition of the masters and the ability of the slaves. A statement of the case, which perhaps is not of much value, was made by a slaveholder in this form: You hire a domestic by the week, or a laborer by the month, for certain wages, with food, lodging, perhaps clothing ; I hire him for the term of life, becoming responsible for him in his decrepitude and old age. Leaving out of view the involuntariness on his part of the arrangement, he gets a good equivalent for his services ; to his risk of being sold, and passing from hand to hand, there is an offset in the perpetual claim which he will have on some owner for maintenance all his days. Whether some of our immigrants would not be willing to enter into such a contract, is a question which many opponents of slavery at the north would not hesitate to answer for them, saying that liberty to beg and to starve is better than to have all your present wants supplied, and a competency for life guarantied, in slavery. Not to discuss the question of the comparative value of liberty in cases in which all good is abstracted, and of slavery when furnished with the comforts of life, it may not be amiss to remind ourselves that the following description from the New York Journal of Commerce cannot be verified within the bounds of the slave States : —

THE MISERIES OF NEW YORK. — A number of hotels and restaurants make a practice of distributing the fragments of food collected from the tables, to the poor, at regular hours, every afternoon. By observing how this is done, any curious person can readily obtain some insight into the miseries of the city. By the same process, a partial cue may be had to the so called " mysteries of New York," which have always afforded a prolific theme for scribblers. The place where these bounties are to be dispensed is indicated some time in advance by the throng of wretched-looking people who eagerly crowd around, with baskets, aprons, &c., in which to bear away the expected gifts. The bloated inebriate, tottering creatures enfeebled by disease, as well as many young girls, acting as agents for others who remain in their own garrets and cellars, — all are represented. On the first appearance of the provisions, which form a complete chowder of bread, meats, pastry, lobster, fish, and vegetables, a general rush is made, which has often to be forcibly repelled. With a large scoop, broken plate, or something of the kind, a quantity of the mixture is thrown into each vessel or other receptacle, extended to receive it, with all possible rapidity, — the crowd meanwhile pressing closer and closer, until again forced into the background. Every device is resorted to in order to secure a double portion. A common trick is, to have a basket placed one side, into which each fresh instalment is deposited, until no more can be procured. Another will have a capacious apron or bag suspended from the waist, secure from observation, while the contents of the extended basket or dish are slyly thrust into it unnoticed. Some, in this manner, obtain the lion's share, while the weak, sick, or decrepit are turned off empty. The scene would bear to be transferred to canvas with an artist's pencil.

SECTION XII. — *Religious Instruction.*

When religious instruction, the pure, simple gospel of Jesus Christ, is extended to our laboring classes generally, adults and children, as fully as it is enjoyed by the slaves in such parts of the south as I visited, an object will be gained of far more intrinsic importance to our national prosperity than all questions relating to slavery.

Probably, in very many places at the south, a larger proportion of the slaves than of the whites have given evidence of being the children of God. The religious condition of the slaves surprises every visitor. The number of communicants among them, in proportion to the whites, is frequently astonishing; for example, in cases known to me, one hundred and fifty blacks to fifty whites, two hundred to twenty, four hundred to one hundred.

In Virginia, the whole number of communicants in the Baptist churches is stated to me, by a Baptist pastor, to be forty-five thousand blacks and fifty thousand whites.

In Savannah, Georgia, in a population of several thousand blacks, more than one third are church members. Three colored pastors, with salaries from eight hundred to a thousand dollars, are supported by subscriptions and pew rents among their own members. More than one

third of the whole number of communicants reported
by the synod of South Carolina are colored people. Of
the three hundred and eighty-four thousand in that State,
one seventh, or more than fifty thousand, are professors
of religion. In 1853, fifteen thousand dollars were contributed by five thousand slaves, in Charleston, to benevolent objects. These statistics, which are a fair sample,
might easily be multiplied, but it is unnecessary. Religion
has gained wonderful ascendency among this people.

I went to their prayer meetings. One of them will
represent the rest. They met in the choir-part of the
gallery, in the evening, once a week. A white brother
presided, as the law requires, and read a portion of
Scripture; but the slaves conducted the meeting. They
came in with their every-day dresses, and each, as he
entered, prostrated himself in prayer. One of them
stood up before the desk, and repeated a hymn, two
lines at a time. At the singing of the last stanza in
each hymn, they all rose; and they invariably repeated
the last two lines of a hymn. They prayed without
being called upon. Such prayers I never heard. There
was nothing during the week that I anticipated with so
much pleasure as the return of that prayer meeting.
Earnestness in manner, overflowing love to God, compassion for their fellow-men every where, gratitude un-
bounded to Christ for his great love wherewith he loved
them, a deep and touching sense of unworthiness, supplica-
tions for mercy and for grace to keep them from sin, all
expressed in original, but frequently ungrammatical, yet
sometimes beautiful and affecting terms, characterized all
their prayers. " O Lord, we prostrate ourselves before
thee on the sinful hands and knees of our poor miserable
bodies and souls." " O Lord, may our hearts all be sot

right to-night; may thy blessed Spirit shine away all our doubts and fears." It was touching to hear one man say, " Bless our dear masters and brothers, who come here to read the Bible to us, and pay so much attention to us, though we ain't that sort of people as can onterpert thy word in all its colors and forms." " O my heavenly Father," said an old man, " I am thy dear child. I know I love thee. Thou art my God, my portion, and nothing else. O my Father, I have no home in this world; my home is very far off. I long to see it. Jesus is there; thou art there; angels, good men are there. I am coming home. I am one day nearer to it."

The hymns being given out from memory, I was much affected in noticing the description of hymns which had been learned. Those by Watts, expressing native depravity and need of regenerating grace, seemed to be favorites, such, for example, as the versifications of the fifty-first psalm: " Show pity, Lord, O Lord, forgive," and, " How sad our state by nature is ! "

I cannot soon forget the looks of one leader, and the impression he and the hymn made upon me. When he repeated two lines at a time, all the meeting joined in singing that hymn — " How oft have sin and Satan strove To rend my soul from thee my God," &c. No one ever seemed to feel the last verse of that hymn more than they — " The gospel bears my spirit up," &c.

I never perceived in their prayers any thing that reminded me of their condition as slaves. They made no allusions to sorrows but those which are spiritual, and they chiefly dwelt upon their temptations. But the love of Christ and heaven were the all-inspiring themes of their prayers and hymns. The pastor of a large colored church, containing many free blacks, told me that he was never reminded by their respective prayers of their respective conditions, as bond or free.

One man prayed with a voice which I never heard surpassed for strength. He had no control over it, so that, when emotions set in with sudden power, they would force it to an amazing pitch, though the sentiment did not always warrant the proportion of stress. I have no question that portions of his prayer could have been heard distinctly across the Connecticut River in any part of its course in a still night. Withal it was musical, and wholly inoffensive.

During the Sabbath, in addition to their opportunities of worship with the whites, a sermon is generally preached to them separately, though the white people are not excluded. The colored men are called upon to offer prayers. The gospel which is preached to them, so far as I heard it, is the same gospel which is preached to us. The only difference between them and us, as to religious instruction, is, they cannot generally read. The white children teach many of them, and the colored children are frequently able to read the Bible. The colored choirs are, of course, able to read.

The laws forbidding their being publicly taught to read are retained in order to be used against those who teach them from motives of interference. But these laws, so far as they restrict the liberty of the citizens in giving instruction, are privately disregarded. A southern member of Congress told me that, in his State, they were generally a dead letter, and that they would be abolished, except that this would expose the people to improper intrusions of teachers and books. In his own case, for example, he was obliged to have men servants that could read, if for no other reason, that they might know the titles of books, superscriptions of letters, and other things, in performing errands or receiving written orders.

Their acquaintance with the word of God is, to a great extent, through oral instruction; yet in all that constitutes Christian excellence, and that knowledge of God which comes directly from him, they have no superiors. A man who has spent a whole life in literary pursuits, and in studying and preaching God's word, listens to those slaves with their comparatively limited acquaintance with the Bible, and feels humble to think that faith and goodness in himself should bear no greater proportion to his knowledge. It is an encouragement to all missionaries among the heathen not to make literature or theoretical instruction even in religion take precedence of simple preaching; there is a knowledge of God imparted to the heart that loves him which far surpasses the instruction of man's wisdom.

These slaves are a rebuke to certain members of churches, men of cultivated minds, literary taste, or general refinement, who are so apt to decline when called upon in religious meetings to make remarks or lead in prayer. The very men who, in many respects, would be most acceptable and useful in these services, generally are made so sensitive by intellectual and social cultivation, that they add nothing to the spiritual interests of a church. It is a sad contrast, a professor in a college, for example, sitting silent for years in the devotional meetings of his church, and a poor slave, who cannot pray grammatically, so wrestling with God in prayer as to make one say of him, " As a prince hast thou power with God and with men." Sometimes the

ordinary low responses of fellow-worshipers in the
Methodist prayer meetings would be excited, by seraphic
expressions in the prayer of a slave brother, to such a
pitch as to raise involuntary shoutings from the whole
meeting, in which I almost wished to join, for the thoughts
expressed were so awakening and elevating that, "or
ever I was aware, my soul made me like the chariots of
Amminadib."

Let us not fail to recognize this indisputable truth,
that the restriction laid upon publicly teaching the
slaves to read has stimulated Christain zeal and benevolence, so that nowhere in our country are greater pains
taken than at the south to instruct the lower classes.
Love to the souls of men will find or make access to
them. The negroes are made to commit passages of
Scripture more generally than in our Sabbath schools;
pains are taken with them which under other circumstances they would not receive.

How frequently at the north, for example, can we
find a scene like this? — a Christian master, surrounded
every morning by fifty laborers in his employ hearing
the Bible read, repeating passages which were given out
the preceding day, singing, and praying, and then going
forth to their labor. Such scenes do occur, and are
becoming more frequent at the south.

A lady of wealth and refinement at the south collects
the mothers among her servants, and forms them into a
maternal association, reads to them on the subject of
education, and encourages them to talk freely with her
and with each other on their duties to their children.
This is only a specimen of the efforts of pious women at
the south in behalf of the slaves.

How wrong it is, in blaming the south for not giving

the Bible to the slaves without restriction, to shut our eyes against these things! Let the tongue be palsied that will justify the shutting up of the book of God from a human being; but virtually this is not done at the south. The negroes are as faithfully and thoroughly instructed in the word of God as any class of people. It is true of them, as the Catechism says, that "the Spirit of God maketh — especially the preaching of the word an effectual means of convicting and converting sinners, and of building them up in holiness and comfort through faith unto salvation." The time must come when every slave can read the Bible; but if one declares that the withholding of it is fatal, it may be asked, How were men saved before the art of printing made copies of the Bible generally accessible? Multitudes of our British ancestors learned the way to heaven who never owned a copy of the Scriptures. Those words, unintelligible to many, in the title pages of Bibles, — " appointed to be read in churches," — show how the people in those days obtained their knowledge of the sacred oracles. The slaves are far better off than they. Large numbers of them can read, and are furnished with the Scriptures, and have as good facility in quoting Scripture in their prayers as Christians generally.

All this is perfectly obvious to any one with a common degree of fairness and candor; but still the whole Bible committed to memory is not so available for spiritual comfort and profit as to have the book in your hand; to have the attention arrested and fixed by the sight of a passage; to look upon the words, and to search the Scriptures, rather than the memory. When the Book of books can be furnished — the New Testament for six cents, and the whole Bible for fifteen — it must be a peremptory reason indeed that will justify us in not bestowing it upon our fellow-men. But we shall resume this topic in another connection.

Of all the situations in which human beings can be placed favorable to the salvation of the soul, under faithful efforts on the part of teachers, it is difficult to conceive of one better suited to this end, and in fact more successful than the relation of these slaves to their Christian masters. It seemed as though human influence went further toward effecting the reception of the gospel by the slaves than in any other cases. Suppose a family of them bound to their master by affection and respect. Whatever he can make appear to their understandings and consciences to be right, he has as much power to enforce upon them as ever falls within the power of moral suasion. So it is, indeed, with pious military and naval commanders, and their soldiers and sailors; subordination, attended with respect and love, opens the widest door for persuasion; and if the numbers of pious slaves are an indication, it must be confessed that slave owners, as a body, have performed their Christian duties to their slaves to a degree which the masters of free apprentices and the employers of free laborers have as yet hardly equaled.

We have thus far looked at the slaves apart from the theory of slavery and from slave laws, and from their liability to suffering by being separated and sold. These features of slavery deserve to be considered by themselves; we can give them and things of that class a more just weight, and view the favorable circumstances of their condition with greater candor. This I have endeavored to do, describing every thing just as it struck me, leaving out of the question the evils of slavery, and abstract doctrines respecting it.

It will not be forgotten that I am describing the appearance of things in a portion of southern society under the highest cultivation. There is, then, a large part of the slaveholding community in which the appearance of the slaves makes agreeable impressions upon a stranger.

Judging of them as you meet them in the streets, see them at work, or at church, or in their prayer meetings and singing meetings, or walking on the Sabbath or holidays, one must see that they are a happy people, their physical condition superior to that of very many of our operatives, far superior to the common Irish people in our cities, and immeasurably above thousands in Great Britain.

Were their condition practically all that many imagine, one thing is certain, viz., insanity would prevail among them to an alarming extent. Corroding care, unmitigated sorrows, fear, and all the natural effects of physical suffering, would produce the same results of insanity with them as with corresponding classes among ourselves. It is well known that the census for 1840 was erroneous with regard to insanity and other diseases, as was ably shown by the American Statistical Association of Boston in a memorial to Congress. Making the largest allowances, it is still true that the comparative number of the insane among the slaves is exceedingly small.

As responsibility, anxiety about the present and future, are the chief enemies to cheerfulness, and, among mental causes, to health, it is obvious that if one can

have all his present wants supplied, with no care about
short crops, the markets, notes payable, bills due, be relieved from the necessity of planning and contriving, all
the hard thinking being done for him by another, while
useful and honorable employment fills his thoughts and
hands, he is so far in a situation favorable to great comfort which will show itself in his whole outer man.
Some will say, " This is the lowest kind of happiness."
Yet it is all that a large portion of the race seek for;
and few, except slaves, obtain it. Thus far I am constrained to say, that the relief which my feelings have
experienced in going to the south and seeing the slaves
at home is very great. Whatever else may be true of
their condition, to whatever perils or sorrows, from
causes not yet spoken of, they may be subjected, I feel
like one who has visited a friend who is sick and reported to be destitute and extremely miserable, but has found
him comfortable and happy. The sickness is there, but
the patient is not only comfortable, but happy, if the ordinary proofs of it are to be taken. We may wonder
that he should be ; we may prove on paper that he can
not be ; but if the colored people of Savannah, Columbia, and Richmond are not, as a whole, a happy people,
I have never seen any.

Much remains to be told. Cases illustrating the opposite of almost every agreeable statement now made
could also be multiplied ; still the things just described
are as represented, and he is not in a healthful state of
mind who cannot appreciate them. Our error has been
in mixing the dark and bright parts of slavery together.
This is wrong. We should never lose sight of distinct moral qualities in character, as we do of different
colors in mixing paint. Let us judge Slavery in this

manner; let us keep her different qualities distinct —
abhor that in her which is evil, rejoice in that which is
good.

It so happened that my observations of things, and
my reflections thus far, as well as those which follow,
occurred very much in the order of my narrative. I
had been at the south four or five weeks before any
thing presented itself to my mind that excited painful
feelings ; but at length it came.

CHAPTER VII.

REVOLTING FEATURES OF SLAVERY.

SECTION I. — *Slave Auctions.*

PASSING up the steps of a court-house in a southern town with some gentlemen, I saw a man sitting on the steps with a colored infant, wrapped in a coverlet, its face visible, and the child asleep.

It is difficult for some who have young children not to bestow a passing look or salutation upon a child; but besides this, the sight before me seemed out of place and strange.

"Is the child sick?" I said to the man, as I was going up the steps.

" No, master; she is going to be sold."

" Sold! Where is her mother?"

" At home, master."

" How old is the child?"

" She is about a year, master."

"You are not selling the child, of course. How comes she here?"

" I don't know, master; only the sheriff told me to sit down here and wait till twelve o'clock, sir."

It is hardly necessary to say that my heart died within me. Now I had found slavery in its most awful feature — the separation of a child from its mother.

" The mother is at home, master." What are her feelings? What were they when she missed the infant? Was it taken openly, or by stealth? Who has done this? What shape, what face had he? The mother is not dead; " the mother is at home, master." What did they do to you, Rachel, weeping and refusing to be comforted?

Undetermined whether I would witness the sale, whether I could trust myself in such a scene, I walked into a friend's law office, and looked at his books. I heard the sheriff's voice, the "public outcry," as the vendue is called, but did not go out, partly because I would not betray the feelings which I knew would be awakened.

One of my friends met me a few minutes after, who had witnessed the transaction.

" You did not see the sale," he said.

" No. Was the child sold? "

" Yes, for one hundred and forty dollars."

I could take this case, so far as I have described it, go into any pulpit or upon any platform at the north, and awaken the deepest emotions known to the human heart, harrow up the feelings of every father and mother, and make them pass a resolution surcharged with all the righteous indignation which language can express. All that any speaker who might have preceded me, supposing the meeting to be one for discussion, might have said respecting the contentment, good looks, happy relations of the slaves, I could have rendered of no avail to his argument by this little incident. No matter what kindness may be exercised in ten thousand instances; a system in which the separation of an infant from its mother is an essential element can not escape reprobation.

On relating what I had seen to some southern ladies, they became pale with emotion; they were silent; they were filled with evident distress. But before remarking upon this case, I will give another. My attention was arrested by the following advertisement: —

" Guardian's Sale.

" Will be sold before the court-house door in ——, on the first Tuesday in May next, agreeably to an order of the ordinary of —— county, the interest of the minors of ——, in a certain negro girl named ——, said interest being three fourths of said negro."

Three fourths of a negro girl to be sold at auction! There was something here which excited more than ordinary curiosity : the application of vulgar fractions to personal identity was entirely new. I determined to witness this sale.

An hour before the appointed time, I saw the. girl sitting alone on the steps of the court-house. She wore a faded but tidy orange-colored dress, a simple handkerchief on her head, and she was barefoot. Her head was resting upon her hand, with her elbow on her knee. I stood unperceived and looked at her. Poor, lonely thing, waiting to be sold on the steps of that court-house! The place of justice is a bleak promontory, from which you look off as upon a waste of waters — a dreary, shoreless waste. What avails every mitigation of slavery ? Had I become a convert to the system, here is enough to counterbalance all my good impressions.

The sheriff arrived at noon, and the people assembled. The purchaser was to have the services of the girl three fourths of the time, a division of property having given some one a claim to one fourth of her appraised value.

The girl was told to stand up. She had a tall, slender form, and was, in all respects, an uncommonly good-looking child.

The bidding commenced at two hundred dollars, and went on in an animated and exciting manner.

The girl began to cry, and wiped her tears with the back of her hand; no one replied to her; the bidding went on; she turned her back to the people. I saw her shoulders heave with her suppressed crying; she said something in a confused voice to a man who sat behind the auctioneer.

When I was young I was drawn, by mingling with some older schoolmates, strongly against my will, and every moment purposing an escape, to see a youth executed for arson. I resolved that I would never look upon such a sight again. But here I was beholding something which moved me as I had not been moved for all these long years.

She was fourteen years old. A few days before I had sent to a child of mine, entering her fourteenth year, a birthday gift. By this coincidence I was led to think of this slave girl with some peculiar feelings. I made the case my own. She was a child to parents, living or dead, whose hearts, unless perverted by some unnatural process, would yearn over her and be distracted by this sight.

Four hundred and forty-five dollars was the last bid, and the man sitting behind the sheriff said to her kindly, " Well, run and jump into the wagon."

A large number of citizens had assembled to witness the sale of this girl; some of them men of education and refinement, humane and kind. On any question of delicacy and propriety, in every thing related to the finest sentiments, I would have felt it a privilege to learn of them. How then, I said to myself as I watched their faces, can you look upon a scene like this as upon an ordinary business transaction, when my feelings are so tumultuous, and all my sensibilities are excruciated? You are not hard-hearted men; you are gentle and generous. In my intercourse with you I have often felt, in the ardor of new friendships, how happy I should be to have you in my circle of immediate friends at home; what ornaments you would be to any circle of Christian friends. Some of you are graduates of Yale College; some of Brown University: you know all that I know about the human heart: I hesitate to believe that I am right and you wrong. If to sell a human being at auction were all which I feel it to be, you must know it as well as I. Yet I cannot yield my convictions. Why do we differ so in our feelings? Instances of private humanity and tenderness have satisfied me that you would not lay one needless burden upon a human being, nor see him suffer without redress. Is it because you are used to the sight that you endure it with composure? or because it is an essential part of a system which you groan under but cannot remove?

To begin with the sale of the infant. During my stay in the place, three or four estimable gentlemen said to me, each in private, "I understand that you saw that infant sold the other day. We are very sorry that you happened to see it. Nothing of the kind ever took place before to our knowledge, and we all feared that it would make an unhappy impression upon you."

The manner in which this was said affected me almost

as much as the thing which had given occasion to it. Southern hearts and consciences, I felt reassured, were no more insensible than mine. The system had not steeled the feelings of these gentlemen; the presence of a northerner, a friend, retaining his private, natural convictions, as they perceived, without unkindness of words or manner, made them look at the transaction with his eyes; every kind and generous emotion was alive in their hearts; they felt that such a transaction needed to be explained and justified.

How could they explain it? How could they justify it? With many, if not with all of my readers, it is a foregone conclusion, as it had been with me, that the case admits of no explanation or justification.

I received, as I said, three or four statements with regard to the case, and this is the substance of them:—

The mother of this infant belonged to a man who had become embarrassed in his circumstances, in consequence of which the mother was sold to another family in the same place, before the birth of the child; but the first owner still laid claim to the child, and there was some legal doubt with regard to his claim. He was disposed to maintain this claim, and it became a question how the child should be taken from him. A legal gentleman, whose name is familiar to the country, told me that he was consulted, and he advised that through an old execution the child should be levied upon, be sold at auction, and thus be removed from him. The plan succeeded. The child was attached, advertised, and offered for sale. The mother's master bought it, at more than double the ratable price, and the child went to its mother.

Nor was this all. In the company of bidders there was a man employed by a generous lady to attend the sale, and see that the infant was restored to its mother. The lady had heard that the sale was to take place, but did not fully know the circumstances, and her purpose was to prevent the child from passing from the parent. Accordingly her agent and the agent of the mother's master were bidding against each other for some time, each with the same benevolent determination to restore the child to its mother.

Rachel was comforted. Rather she had had no need of being comforted, for the sheriff was in this case to be her avenger and protector. Here was slavery restoring a child to its mother; here was a system which can deal in unborn children, redressing its own wrong. Moreover, the law which forbids the sale of a child under five years was violated, in order to keep the child with its mother. The man who had the claim on the unborn child was from Connecticut.

Had I not known the sequel of the story, what a thrilling, effective appeal could I have made at the north by the help of this incident. Then what injustice I should have inflicted upon the people of that place; what stimulus might I have given to the rescue of a fugitive slave; what resuscitation to the collapsing vocabulary of epithets. How might I have helped on the dissolution of the Union; how have led half our tribes to swear that they would have war with the rest forever, when in truth the men and women who had done this thing had performed one of the most tender and humane actions, and did prevent, and, if necessary, with their earthly all, (for I knew them well,) would have prevented that from ever taking place to which, in my ignorance and passion, I should have sworn that I could bear witness — an infant taken from its mother's breast and sold.

The "three fourths" of the girl were bought by the owner of the other fourth, who already had possession of her. The sale took place that he might be her sole owner. That word which followed the sale, "Well, run and jump into the wagon," was music to the child. I understood afterward why she turned her back to the crowd, and looked at the man who sat behind the sheriff. He was her master, and he owned her mother; the girl heard the bidding from the company, and heard her master bidding; the conflict she understood; she was at stake, as she felt, for life; it took some time for the bidding to reach four hundred dollars; hope deferred made her heart sick; she turned and kept her eye on her master, to see whether he would suffer himself to be defeated. He sat quietly using his knife upon a stick, like one whose mind was made up; the result of the sale in his favor excited no new feeling in him; but the ready direction, "Well, run and jump into the wagon," was as much as to say, I have done what I meant to do when I came here.

I did not see "Jacob," forty-five years of age, well recommended, who was advertised to be sold at the same time and place. The sheriff announced that the sale of Jacob was merely to perfect a title. There was only one bid, therefore — six hundred dollars; the owner thus going through a form to settle some legal question.

We are all ready to inquire as to the views and feelings of good men at the south with regard to the sale of slaves at auction. I felt great curiosity to know how some of the best of men regarded it.

1. They say that very many of the slaves advertised with full descriptions, looking like invitations to buy, are merely legal appointments to determine claims, settle

estates, without any purpose to let the persons offered for sale pass from the families to which they belong.

It was some relief to know as much as this. At home and at the south advertisements in southern papers of negroes for sale at auction, describing them minutely, have often harrowed our feelings. The minute description, they say, is, or may be, a legal defence in the way of proof and identification.

2. However trying a public sale may be to the feelings of the slave, they say that it is for his interest that the sale should be public.

The sale of slaves at auction in places where they are known — and this is the case every where except in the largest cities — excites deep interest in some of the citizens of that place. They are drawn to the sale with feelings of personal regard for the slaves, and are vigilant to prevent unprincipled persons from purchasing and carrying them away, and even from possessing them in their own neighborhood. I know of citizens combining to prevent such men from buying, and of their contributing to assist good men and women in purchasing the servants at prices greatly increased by such competition. In all such cases the law requiring and regulating public sales and advertisements of sales prevents those private transfers which would defeat the good intentions of benevolent men. It is an extremely rare case for a servant or servants who have been known in town to be removed into hands which the people of the place generally would not approve.

The sale of a negro at public auction is not a reckless, unfeeling thing in the towns at the south, where the subjects of the sale are from among themselves. In settling estates, good men exercise as much care with regard to the disposition of the slaves as though they were providing homes for white orphan children; and that too when they have published advertisements of slaves in such connections with horses and cattle, that, when they are read by a northerner, his feelings are excruciated. In hearing some of the best of men, such as are found in all communities, largely intrusted with the settlement of estates, men of extreme fairness and incorruptible integrity, speak of the word " chattel" as applied to slaves, it is obvious that this unfeeling law term has no counterpart in their minds, nor in the feelings of the community in general.

Slaves are allowed to find masters and mistresses who will buy them. Having found them, the sheriffs' and administrators' sales must by law be made public, the persons must be advertised, and every thing looks like an unrestricted offer, while it is the understanding of the company that the sale has really been made in private.

Sitting in the reading-room of a hotel one morning, I saw a colored woman enter and courtesy to a gentleman opposite.

" Good morning, sir.   Please, sir, how is Ben?"

"Ben — he is very well.   But I don't know you."

"Ben is my husband.   I heard you were in town, and I want you to buy me.   My mistress is dead these three weeks, and the family is to be broken up."

"Well, I will buy you.   Where shall I inquire?"

All this was said and done in as short a time as it takes to read it; but this woman was probably obliged by law, in the settlement of the estate, to be advertised and described.

All these things go far to mitigate our feelings with

regard to the sale of slaves at auction in many cases. But even with regard to these cases, no one who is not used to the sight will ever see it but with repugnance and distress.

I walked with a gentleman, esteemed and honored by his fellow-citizens, and much intrusted with the settlement of estates. I knew that he would appreciate my feelings, and I disclosed them. I asked him if there were no other way of changing the relations of slaves in process of law, except by exposing them, male and female, at auction, on the court-house steps. I told him how I felt on seeing the girl sold, and that the knowledge subsequently of the satisfactory manner in which the case was disposed of did not make me cease to feel unhappy. I could not bear to see a fellow-being made a subject of sale, even in form; and I wondered that any one could look upon it with composure, or suffer it to be repeated without efforts to abolish it.

His reply was, for substance, that so far as he and the people of his town were concerned, no case of hardship in the disposal of a slave had ever occurred there, to his knowledge; that he had settled a large number of estates, and in every case had disposed of the servants in ways satisfactory to themselves; that he had prevented certain men from bidding upon them; that he had prevailed on others not to buy, because he and the servants were unwilling to have these men for their masters; and, therefore, that the question was practically reduced to the expediency of the form of transfer, viz., by public vendue.

He repeated what I have said of the desirableness that the sale or transfer should be public; whether in a room, or on steps, was unimportant, only that every public outcry was ordained to be made at the court-house. He also said that the slaves, knowing that the sale was a mere form, and that they were already disposed of, did not in such cases suffer to the degree which strangers supposed.

It was evident, from all that he said, that he transfused his own kind, benevolent feelings, and those of his fellow-citizens over every sale within the limits of his town, and could not, therefore, see it with a northerner's eyes and heart.

The forms of law are as inconsiderate of our feelings as though they were acts of barbarians. A sheriff's sale of house furniture in the dwelling of a man who has fallen from opulence into insolvency is like the wheel of torture, that breaks every bone and joint one by one. The auctioneer, with precious household treasures, keepsakes, memorials of dear departed friends, in one hand, and a crumpled newspaper for a hammer in the other, seems to be a most unfeeling man; but he is not so; it is law, of which he is the exponent, that is so terrible.

No human being, innocent of crime, ought to be subjected to the rack of being offered for sale, nor ought fellow-creatures ever to behold that sight. It will be done away. Reproachful words, however, will not hasten the removal of it.

I once stated the subject to a friend in this form: We cannot expect that servants can abide in a house forever. Death breaks up their relations, and they must have other masters. Allowing all you say of their being necessarily a serving class, why not always give them a voice in changing these relations? This is done uniformly in some of your towns. I could name one in which no slave has been disposed of otherwise for ten years at least, except in cases of refractory and trouble-some persons.

Then let opportunity be given for private inquiry and examination ; let the transfer be made without obliging the slave to be present, and this will approximate as far as possible to the method of obtaining servants at employment offices.

At the Christmas holidays, some of the southern cities and towns are alive with the negroes, in their best attire, seeking employment for the year to come, changing places, and having full liberty to suit themselves as to their employers. The characters and habits of all the masters and mistresses are known and freely discussed by them.

So, instead of selling a family at auction upon the death of a master, it is often the case that letters are written for them to people in different States, where they may happen to have acquaintances, perhaps to relatives of the master's family, known and beloved, asking them to buy ; and thus the family is disposed of to the satisfaction of all concerned. Wherever kindness prevails, the evils of slavery can be made to disappear as much as from any condition, especially where the servants are worthy.

But then there are cases in which the feelings of the slave are wantonly disregarded, and the owners make no distinction, and are incapable of making any, between a negro and a mule.

Then there are slaves who are vicious and disagreeable, whom their owners are glad to sell out of their sight, as other men are glad to be rid of certain apprentices or refractory children, and feel happier the greater the distance to which they remove.

Again, men in pecuniary straits, in the hands of a broker or sheriff, do things which excruciate themselves as much as their slaves. Thus, in part, the domestic slave trade is maintained.

Section II. — *Domestic Slave Trade.*

A southern physician described to me a scene in the domestic slave trade. He touched at a landing-place in a steamer, and immediately a slave coffle was marched on board. Men, women, and children, about forty in all, two by two, an ox chain passing through the double file, and a fastening reaching from the right and left hands of those on either side of the chain, composed what is called a *slave coffle.* Some colored people were on the wharf, who seemed to be relatives and friends of the gang. Such shrieks, such unearthly noises, as resounded above the escape of steam, my informant said can not be described. There were partings for life, and between what degrees of kindred the nature of the cries were probably a sign.

When the boat was on her way, my informant fell into conversation with a distinguished planter, with regard to the scene which they had just witnessed. They deplored it as one of the features of a system which they both mourned over, and wished to abolish, or at least correct, till no wrong, no pain, should be the fruit of it which is not incidental to every human lot.

While they were discussing the subject, the slave-dealer heard their talk, came up, and made advances to shake hands with the planter. The gentleman drew back, and said, " Sir, I consider you a disgrace to human nature." He poured scorn and indignation upon him.

He spoke the feelings of the south generally. Negro traders are the abhorrence of all flesh. Even their descendants, when they are known, and the property acquired in the traffic, have a blot upon them. I never knew a deeper aversion to any class of men; it is safe to say, that generally it is not surpassed by our feelings toward foreign slave traders.

They go into the States where the trade is not prohibited by law, find men who are in want of money, or a master who has a slave that is troublesome, and for the peace of the plantation that slave is sold, sometimes at great sacrifice; and there are many of whom, under pecuniary pressure, it is not always difficult to purchase.

There are some men whose diabolical natures are gratified by this traffic — passionate, cruel, tyrannical men, seeking dominion in some form to gratify these instincts. The personal examinations which they make, and the written descriptions which they give, of slaves whom they buy, are sometimes disgusting in the extreme. It is beyond explanation that good men at the south do not clamor against this thing, till the transfer of every human being, if he must be a slave, is made with all the care attending the probate of a will.

The charge of vilely multiplying negroes in Virginia, is one of those exaggerations of which this subject is full, and is reduced to this — that Virginia, being an old State, fully stocked, the surplus black population naturally flows off where their numbers are less.

I heard this conversation at the breakfast house of a southern railroad. As several of us were warming ourselves at the fire, one of the passengers said to the keeper of the house, —

" Where is Alonzo now? "

" He is in Alabama."

" I thought he had come back."

" Well, he was to come back some time ago; but they keep sending him so many negroes to sell, he can't leave."

Alonzo is probably a negro trader of the better sort; a mere agent or factor. If slaves are to be sold, there must be men to negotiate with regard to them; these are not all of the vilest sort; yet their occupation is abhorred.

The separation of families seems to be an inevitable feature of slavery, as it exists at present. If a man is rich and benevolent, he will provide for his servants, and tax himself to support them, let their number be never so great, buying one plantation after another, chiefly to employ his people. But the time will come when he must die, and his people are deprived of his protection. No one child, perhaps, can afford to keep them together; perhaps he has no children; then they must take their chance of separations to the widest borders of the slave States. But here individual kindness mitigates sorrow and distress. The owner of several plantations at the south, with no children, has made his slaves his heirs, on condition that they remove to Liberia.

It seems to be taken for granted that to be sold is inevitably to pass from a good to an inferior condition. This is as much a mistake as it would be to assert the same of changes on the part of domestic servants in the free States. There are as good masters as those whose death makes it necessary to scatter the slaves of an estate. The change itself is not necessarily an evil.

We must remember that slaves are not the only inhabitants, nor slave families the only families, in the land, that are scattered by the death of others. Sometimes the demand seems to be that slaves should be kept together at all events, and separations never be permitted. This is absurd, upon the least reflection. No one ought to demand or expect for them an experience better or worse than the common lot of men. Let the slaves share with us in the common blessings and calamities of divine providence. What would become of our families of five or ten children should their parents die? Can we keep our children about us always? Do none but black children go to the ends of the Union and become settled there? How many white people there are that do this, who — deplorable truth! — cannot read and write, and seldom if ever hear of their relatives from whom they are separated. Let us not require too much of slavery. Let us not insist that the slaves shall never be separated, nor their families broken up; but let it be done as in the course of nature every where, with no more pain, nor pain of any other kind, than must accrue to those who depend upon their own efforts for a living.

Facts connected with this part of the subject have given me deep respect and sympathy for those slaveholders who, from the number of instances which have come to my knowledge, it is evident are by no means few, that suffer hardship and loss in their efforts to keep the members of their slave families together. Our knowledge of distressing cases, and the indisputable truth that slavery gives the power of disposal to the owner at his will, no doubt leads us to exaggerate the number of cases in which suffering is unjustly inflicted. While we are sure to hear of distressing cruelties, ten thousand acts of kindness are not mentioned. These can not compensate, however, for the liability to abuse which there is in authority almost absolute; but still let us discriminate when we bring charges against a whole community, and let us consider how far the evils complained of are inseparable, not only from a system which is felt to be a burden, but also from human nature in every condition.

As was remarked with regard to sales by auction, it is in vain to expect that painful separations of families in a wanton manner, or by stress of circumstances, can wholly cease, in the present system. It is indeed a burdensome system, destroying itself by its own weight, unless relieved by some of those unnatural and violent expedients. It is deplored for this and other reasons by multitudes at the south, whose voices we shall hear as soon as our relations as north and south are such as will allow them to speak. In the mean time, public sentiment is fast correcting abuses under the system; and not only so, but through its influence and the power of Christian love, the condition of families and individuals among the slaves is becoming here and there as free from evil as human nature permits in a dependent condition.

CHAPTER VIII.

REVOLTING FEATURES OF SLAVERY — CONTINUED.

SECTION III. — *Homes of the Slaves.*

THE homes of the slaves is a topic of deep interest, bearing in a vital manner upon the system. It can hardly be said in general that slaves have regularly constituted homes. Husbands and wives, in a large proportion of cases, belong to different masters, and reside on separate plantations, the husband sometimes walking several miles, night and morning, to and from his family, and many of them returning home only on Saturday afternoon. In cities, also, husbands and wives most commonly belong to different families. Laboring apart, and having their meals apart, the bonds of domestic life are few and weak. A slave, his wife, and their children, around that charmed centre, a family table, with its influences of love, instruction, discipline, humble as they necessarily would be, yet such as God had given them, are too seldom seen. To encourage and protect their homes generally would be in effect to put an end to slavery as it is.

It was remarked to me by an eminent and venerable physician at the south, that maternal attachments in slave mothers are singularly shortlived. Their pain and grief at the sale of their children, their jealousy, their self-sacrificing efforts for them, are peculiar; but they are easily supplanted. The hen, and even the timid partridge, is roused when her young are in danger, and her demonstrations of affection then are unsurpassed. Yet in a few weeks she will treat her offspring as strangers. Maternal instincts in slave mothers (my friend observed) were more like this than the ordinary parental feelings of white people.

I told him that this disclosed to me one of the most affecting illustrations of slavery, and that I needed not to ask him for his explanation of it. Every one can see, not only the probability, but the cause, of this limited parental affection. From the first moment of maternal solicitude, the idea of property on the part of the owner in the offspring is connected with the maternal instinct. It grows side by side with it, becomes a neutralizing element, prevents the inviolable links of natural affection from reaching deep into the heart. We need no slave auctions or separations of families to make us feel the inherent, awful nature of the present system of slavery, in view of this illustration.

Some use it in mitigation of the alleged wrongfulness of separating mothers and young children. Human nature refuses to hear one who is capable of using such an argument.

The same day that my friend made his remark to me, I had an accidental confirmation of it in the conversation of an intelligent landlord, who was telling me of the recent lamentable death of an old slave mother who had nursed him and all his brothers and sisters. His mother said to the dying woman, " How do you feel about leaving your children?" for she had several, who were still young. " O missis," she said, " you will take care of them; I don't mind them. I don't want to leave you, missis, and your Charley and Ann. What will they do without me, little dears?" The gentleman mentioned it as an affecting illustration, as it certainly is, of the disinterested affection in these colored servants; but I felt that there was something back of all this. Slavery had loosened the natural attachments of this woman to her offspring, and those attachments had sought and found objects to grow upon in the children of another. There must be something essentially wrong in a system which thus interferes with the nature which God has made.

The drapery of words is hardly sufficient, perhaps, to clothe an idea which a slave mother in one of the best of Christian families expressed; but she was deprecating the possibility of being a mother again. She said, " You feel when your child is born that you can't have the bringing of it up."

One evening, in a prayer meeting of slaves, the white brother who presided read the chapter in Matthew containing the Lord's Prayer, and asked me to make some remarks. I alluded to the Lord's Prayer, which had just been read, and was proceeding to remark upon portions of it. I found myself embarrassed, however, at once, in speaking about that overwhelming name of love — Our Father, who art in heaven ; for it flashed upon me, these slaves, although they have the spirit of sons, although they cry " Abba, Father," as I seldom ever heard other Christians use the name, can not appreciate any illustrations of it which I may draw from earthly parentage; they know the thing; the illustration they cannot fully appreciate, for in effect the slave has no father. He more frequently remembers his mother; but who was his father? His knowledge of him is far less frequent.

The annihilation by slavery, to a great extent, of the father in the domestic relations of the slaves, is inseparable from it, as it exists at present.

Take a further illustration. I was in a large colored Sabbath school. The superintendent at the close gave the scholars a kind word of exhortation to this effect: " Now, children, I want to repeat what I have said to you so often; you must all try to be good children, wherever you are, remembering that you are never out of God's sight. If you love and obey him, if you are good children at home, what a comfort you will be to your" [I expected the words *fathers* and *mothers*] " masters and mistresses." I felt as when I have heard the earth fall upon a stranger's coffin; it was all correct, all kind; but the inability to use those names, the perfect naturalness with which other names came in to fill the place of *father* and *mother*, brought to my heart the truth, the slaves generally have no homes.

Living disintegrated as they now do, it is easier to transfer them from place to place. Thus the prevalence of homes in slavery, regularly constituted and defended, would soon make slavery almost impracticable, or reduce it to almost an unobjectionable form. The red sandstone soil in parts of the south is destroyed, large sections being washed away, leaving a hard, clayey surface. That beautiful feature of New England, our northern grass, does not prevail there, with its thick-set roots to bind the soil. Homes among the slaves would be to them what the grass would be to the soil.

Separated as they necessarily are under the present system, the relations of husbands and wives are not so inviolable as they otherwise would be. Marriage among the slaves is not a civil contract; it is formed and continues by permission of the masters; it has no binding force, except as moral principle preserves it; and it is subject, of course, to the changes of fortune on the part of the owners. This is the theory; but humane and benevolent hearts in every community combine to modify its operation; yet there are cases of hardship over which they are compelled to weep, and very many of them do weep as we should in their places; still the system remains, and now and then asserts its awful power.

There is a lad at the south about fifteen years old, whose form, features, manners, and general aptitude interested me in him very much, whose mother has had three husbands sold within three years. To see him while talking throw himself from one seat to another, and upon the floor, in the abandonment of grief, with wailings cursing his birth, it would seem is enough to prevent any stranger from falling in love with slavery. In these three cases, straitened circumstances compelled the sales.

Yet the cases of violent separation of husband and wife are not so many as the voluntary and criminal separations by the parties themselves. This, after all, is the chief evil connected with the looseness of domestic ties in slavery. Conjugal love among the slaves is not invariably the poetical thing which amateurs of slaves sometimes picture it; for there are probably no more happy conjugal unions among the slaves than among the whites.

At the spring term, this year, of the court in one New England State, there were eighty-three applications for divorce; thirty-three were granted, seven were refused, and forty-three were reserved for consideration. In another State, at the same term, there were seventy-three applications; forty-two were granted, four were refused, and three were settled; the rest were continued. Probably in no slave State were there more voluntary separations of husbands and wives among the slaves than in some of the New England States that could be specified for the same period. The only difference is, the slave does not go to court for his divorce. He absents himself from his cabin, or procures another master; or, belonging to the same master with his wife, and being unwilling to live within possible hearing of her, he flees to the north. If he has a good degree of address, he can rouse up the deep philanthropy of freemen, like a ground-swell of the sea, in overwhelming pity and compassion for him; while the only unhappiness, after all, in his particular case, was, that he could not have laws to countenance and defend him in putting away his wife, who had committed no crime, and marrying another. The people of those communities whose laws of divorce are of questionable morality, will not, of course, throw the first stone at the south, for that looseness in the domestic relations of slaves which allows so many voluntary separations.

I have conversed with pastors of churches at the south on this subject. Human nature is the same among the whites as among the blacks, but the mode of life among the slaves gives peculiar facilities for vice; the separation of husbands and wives by sale encourages them to think lightly of mutual obligations, and conjugal faithfulness for the time yields easily to temptation. They are faithfully preached to from the pulpit on the subject, religious restraints are felt, the expectation of honorable marriage has influence, and it is libelous to say that there are not very many in the churches who keep themselves pure. Still it is universally confessed that one prominent evil of slavery is seen in this. The pastor of a colored church says to me, in a letter, " The violation of the law of chastity among my congregation is the besetting sin. Of the three hundred and seventeen persons excluded during a certain period, as appears by our church books, two hundred were for adultery." But this is a congregation in which an unusually large proportion are free blacks. There are restraints imposed upon slaves in this particular, in many cases, which, of course, are not felt by those who are free. Knowing, as ministers in cities are apt to do, the statistics of crime, it would be gratifying if we could assert that our northern cities are examples to the south in all goodness. After reading all that has ever been written respecting the sale and purchase of " yellow girls," and the extent to which the sin alluded to prevails at the south, you may obtain from any experienced policeman in one of our cities disclosures which will give exercise to virtuous abhorrence and indignation as great as the statistics of sin and misery elsewhere can excite, unless, indeed, wickedness at home fails to exert the enchantment which belongs to other men's sins. What if there were some way in which this iniquity in the free States proclaimed itself as it does through complexion at the south ?

" Some men's sins are open beforehand, going before to judgment, and some men they follow after."

Christian public sentiment at the south revolts at the sale of one's own children as instinctively as at the north, and points the finger at this abomination.

SECTION IV. — *Domestic Evils deplored by the Whites.*

There are evils pertaining to slavery of which none are so well aware as those who are subjected to them; and therefore the free and candid declaration of the people at the south upon this part of the subject is far more convincing and satisfactory than our theoretical reasonings.

They complain of the injurious effect of slave labor upon the soil, there being no motives with the slave to improve or preserve it; but this is too obvious a topic to require a single remark.

Labor performed wholly by menial persons becomes disreputable in the eyes of children. Those who can afford to educate their children to live in affluence are not oppressed by this evil as others are whose children eschew trades and every thing requiring manual labor, and, irrespective of talent, must resort to the army and navy and the learned professions for a living. Society is happier where a portion of its own talent and enter-prise is employed in the mechanic arts. It is the provi-dential arrangement that invention shall be the offspring of labor, they who work being those ordinarily who con-fer upon the world the fruits of genius Slaves invent little or nothing. The healthful stimulus of necessity finds few heads or hands at the south among the labor-ing class, almost every thing necessary to quicken and help labor being imported. It is a serious evil which parents in slave States feel, that they do not enjoy the privilege of employing the talents and aiding the constitutions of some of their children by addicting them at home to the useful arts, which abound where labor is honorable and is rewarded. Temptations to vice, and the mischiefs of an aimless, idle life, are the source of great solicitude and pain to many southern parents with regard to their sons.

We greatly err when we make this an occasion for reproach. There is a way of taunting the south with this and other inseparable inconveniences and evils of their state of society which is unkind. Their reply might well be, " God has given us 'a south land,' as Caleb gave to his daughter. O that he could give us also, as she requested, 'springs of water.' Sources of refreshment and comfort which you at the north enjoy are, some of them, withheld from us."

Were it not for the din and clamor of northern invectives against slavery, we should hear more distinctly the candid expressions of our southern friends with regard to evils in the system.

They tell us — and indeed every one sees it — that slave labor is in many cases oppressively expensive, and the more so in proportion to the conscientiousness and kindness of the owners. It takes more hands to do the same amount of work than with us; the servants are hearty, and great consumers, frequently costing more for their food than the rest of the family ; and some of them could be dispensed with, but they came into the family in ways, perhaps, which make their owners unwilling to put them away. This is an evil in slavery of which we at the north have very little idea, and it does much to disabuse a spectator of wrong impressions made by his associations with the word *slavery* and *slave*. One case out of many in every southern town may be mentioned, of a matron, a widow, who, during her husband's life, was in easy circumstances; but he having left her with some colored women and their children, she receives boarders that she may have means to support these blacks, being unwilling to sell them, but expecting the time when she can place them in advantageous situations. She would pass at the north under the name of "slaveholder," with all the peculiar associations with that name in the minds of many. It was affecting to hear her say, " If our friends at the north would devise ways in which we could dispose of these poor people for their good, I should then no longer be a servant of servants."

There are, probably, few who would not abstractly prefer free labor; but what shall be done with the blacks? There has never been a time in the history of our discussions on this subject, when, if the south had expressed her willingness to part with the slaves, we at the north could have agreed in what way they should have been disposed of. Who has ever proposed a plan of relief which could in a good measure unite us? What shall be done with the blacks? On the evils of slavery all are well informed. But as to this essential question we get no light.

TAKING all the favorable features and all the evils of southern slavery together simply as to their bearing upon the slave, it appears that, leaving out of view the liabilities to separation, to be a slave at the south is an evil or not according to the character or habits of the master. The master or mistress can make the relation of a slave the very best on earth for one who must be dependent. One can not be long at the south, and not see for himself that the perfection of human happiness in a serving class is found among certain slaves. There is nothing that approaches to it except the relation of certain servants and dependants of noble families in Great Britain; but at the south the relation and the happiness do not depend upon family and wealth; every householder may be a master or mistress to whom it will be a privilege to belong. Instances come to mind of servants in whose condition nothing is wanting to promote happiness in this world and preparation for the next; and the only source of disquietude in such cases you will hear thus expressed: "Master may die, and then I shall have to be free. I have laid up money, and am mentioned in the will, and my free papers are made out." Such servants sometimes select new masters, and prevail on them to buy them, preferring the feeling of protection, the gratification of loving and serving a white person, to abstract liberty.

Then there is another side to this picture. It is in the power of a master or mistress to make the condition of the slave a perpetual sorrow. It would be well if some men, and women too, could be debarred by law from having authority over a human being. One looks with pity even upon the animal that belongs to them. Imperative, fierce, threatening in their tones, petulant and cruel in their dispositions, capricious and contradictory in their orders, and full of scolding, the word and blow coming together, they wear out the patience of their servants. No wonder that the slaves of such men and women run away, that white boys in similar circumstances betake themselves to the sea, and girls elope or go to service, as a refuge from such dispositions and tongues. A certain distinguished slave owner seriously entertains the desire, for which his friends banter him, that every one proposing to be a slaveholder shall bring certificates of good temper, and be examined. To one who was a most thorough lover of the system of slavery I put the question, in a favorable moment, " What, in your view, is the greatest objection that can be made to slavery?" " O," said he, " this irresponsible power. You can not prevent its abuse while human nature is what it is. Good and kind men and women can make a slave happier than he could be any where; but certain masters and mistresses of slaves are the worst of tyrants."

There are some men to whom a negro is merely an ox or an ass. They buy, sell, work, treat, talk about, their " niggers " as about cattle — hard, sharp, vulgar men of whom we have a good idea in the following extract from the journal of a traveler in Texas, which appeared some time since in a newspaper, and which I read and verified at the south. The writer says, —

" I remember, now, one gentleman of property in ——, sitting with us one night, ' spitting in the fire,' and talking about cotton. Bad luck he had had — only four and a half bales to the hand; couldn't account for it — bad luck; and next year he didn't reckon nothing else but that there would be a general war in Europe, and then he'd be in a pretty fix, with cotton down to four cents a pound. Curse those Turks! If he thought there would be a general war, he would take every —— nigger he'd got right down to New Orleans, and sell them for what they'd bring. They'd never be so high again as they are now, and if there should come a general war they wouldn't be worth half so much next year. There always were some infernal rascals some where in the world trying to prevent an honest man from getting a living. O, if they got to fighting, he hoped they'd eat each other up. They just ought to be, all of them — Turks, and Russians, and Prussians, and Dutchmen, and Frenchmen — all of them just be put in a bag together, and slung ——. That's what he'd do with them."

It will generally be expected that punishment by whipping should be mentioned among the revolting features of slavery. In a well-regulated southern household, as in a well-ordered family of children, or a good school, the rod is out of sight. It is seldom alluded to ; threatenings are rare ; but the knowledge on the part of each servant, child, and pupil, that there is a punishment in reserve for the last resort, will have a salutary effect. Southern ladies, when they meet insolence or disobedience in their slaves, have not our easy means of relief in dismissing them at once, and repairing to the intelligence offices for others. They must have them punished, or they must continue to bear with them, as they often do, with long and exemplary patience, shrinking as we should from subjecting them to punishment ; or they must sell them, as incorrigible, to the slave trader, which is far worse than chastisement, however severe. In good hands this power is exercised without abuse.

This power is also in the hands of the cruel and unprincipled, and is fearfully abused. Slaves, however, are not the only subjects of these cruelties, nor masters of slaves the only transgressors. The following extract taken from a newspaper, with remarks upon it by a southern editor, are given here partly for the sake of a comment upon the strictures of the editor. Some of his remarks are just. It is the legislature of a free State which is referred to.

" The —— legislature has before it an investigation into the conduct of ——, of the state prison, who is accused of cruelty toward a colored prisoner whom he suspected of stealing from him three hundred dollars. It is alleged he deprived him of his clothing, and confined him in a dungeon without a bed for sixteen days. At three separate times he was brought out, stripped to his skin, and whipped with a cat till his back was cut to pieces, and the blood made to flow from the wounds. In this condition he was put back into his dark, damp, cold cell, without a bed or particle of bedclothes, to pass three days and nights as best he could. At the end of that time he was again taken out, whipped as before, and this repeated for three times; and when last put back, he was told that he would be confined and whipped every day till the expiration of his sentence, if he did not confess."

A southern editor says, with regard to this paragraph, —

" It were an easy matter to cull from every northern mail that reaches us accounts of individual instances of cruelty and brutality. It would not be venturing too far to say, that, for every three hundred and sixty-five days in the year, the New York, Philadelphia, and Boston papers contain the particulars of some inhuman exercise of authority, some outrageous case of arson or burglary, or some horrible murder of a wife by her husband, or of a husband by his wife, of a child by its parent, or of a parent by the child. We might make out a catalogue of sins and offences almost sufficient to overwhelm these cities with the terrible fate of Sodom and Gomorrah, should the divine justice subject them to the same conditions imposed upon those ancient sinks of iniquity. We might even arrive at the conclusion that there was something radically wrong and corrupt in the framework of society where enormities of the most frightful and disgusting character are of such frequent occurrence. * * * We all know that the most heinous violations of law, at the north as well as at the south, are seldom followed by an execution. We know,

further, that the disgusting details of a divorce case have
been known to divide public attention in New York with
a revolution in France, and that the brutal pugilist Tom
Hyer, on his return from his victory over Yankee Sullivan,
was paraded up Broadway in an open carriage.

" We do not choose, however, to abuse the position we
occupy as a public journalist. We know there are just
as good people at the north as there are at the south, or
any where else. We know there are violators of law in
all countries and under all circumstances of life, and that
it is both wrong and untruthful to charge their crimes upon
the communities in which they reside, or upon any one of
the institutions with which they are surrounded. Freedom
is not responsible for the sins of the north, nor is slavery
amenable for the transgressions of the south. Whatever
is wrong in either section should be ascribed to the proper
cause — to that perverted nature which led Cain to take
the life of his brother, and which has filled the earth with
all the evil and woe which have afflicted it from that day
until this."

Now, suppose that the papers of the south should have
each a corps of reporters to pry every where for stirring
items in connection with slavery, and that those papers
should have the same inducements to publish them which
our papers have to report the last instances of abuse and
crime here.

We will not say that the balance in favor of the south
would be changed; but the suggestion will not be gain-
said, that to make the cases parallel, the means of information in the two cases must be the same.

Passing by a plantation, I saw a white man standing
in a field near the road, with his arms folded, and a large
whip in his hand. A little farther on, I came to a row
of fifteen or twenty negroes, hoeing industriously, without lifting their heads to look at those who were going
by. Had I told this overseer how I felt on seeing him,
he would probably have replied, that my feelings were
northern prejudices; that he never strikes the negroes,

and is on good terms with them ; that his whip is partly
in self-defence in case of need, and partly to enforce, by
its bare presence, his orders, in refractory cases, should
they occur.   But he was a revolting sight.

Many planters do not employ white overseers, but
use some of the hands in their stead, paying them for
this responsibility.   Touching instances of faithfulness
are related of these colored head men.   The white overseers have it in their power, of course, to perpetrate
many tyrannical and cruel acts ; but we must not suppose that southern masters are indifferent to wrongs and
outrages committed against their slaves.   There is a
public sentiment to which they are amenable ; a cruel,
neglectful master is marked and despised ; and if cruel
or neglectful by proxy, he does not escape reprobation.
It was not unusual to hear one say of another, " I have
been told that he does not use his people well."   This
is a brand upon a man which he and his family are made
to feel deeply.   But this is true only of certain states
of society.

Slaveholding, like every relation, is a net which gath-
ers of every kind.   There are elements in it, at the
south, fitted to promote the highest happiness and welfare, temporal and spiritual, of the negro ; and it can
make him perfectly miserable.   Many things charged
against slavery are chargeable to ' construction account '
in human nature.

The most common expression at the south, with regard to slavery, is, " It is a great curse."   An intelligent
gentleman, a slaveholder, said, in answer to a question,
that unquestionably four-fifths of the people of his State,
one of the oldest slave States, would be entirely free from

it were it possible. It is well known that several slave States have been upon the borders of emancipation. In the public debates which have been had in Virginia at different times on this subject are to be found some of the most able and thorough arguments against slavery. Here is one illustration, among many which might be given, of antislavery feeling at the south, just previous to the recent excitement with regard to Nebraska and Kansas. The Providence Journal says, —

SLAVERY IN WESTERN VIRGINIA. — A good deal of excitement has been caused in Wheeling by the course of the Times newspaper in that city, openly favoring the abolition of slavery. There are few slaves in Western Virginia, and the country is not adapted to slave labor; but the sentiment of the State, its feelings, prejudices, and traditions are all so intensely favorable to slavery, that it requires no little boldness for a man to stand up in the midst of all these unfavorable influences, and speak the plain truth. The boldness of the Times in doing so was attempted to be rebuked by a public meeting, called to condemn the abolitionism of that print. The meeting was large; the resolutions condemning the Times were voted down, and others were substituted approving of the honesty and independence of its course. The following is the manner in which the Times discusses the question of slavery, and these are the sentiments which the people read, and which they defend the editor for publishing: —

" We are in favor of taking the earliest possible means of getting rid of slavery in the State of Virginia, with justice to the master, safety to the State, and comfort and convenience to the laboring population now in it.

" We desire it because it has retarded the progress of the people since it became a State, impoverishing its inhabitants, reducing its population, and staying the development of the vast natural resources that abound in the State, to a greater extent than in any other State in the Union. Had it not been for slavery, Norfolk would now be what New York and Philadelphia are. Norfolk has the best harbor in the Union, and the natural soil that extends from the coast to the Blue Ridge is among the best in the country.

Had that institution not existed there, or if it should be removed, how long would it be before Norfolk would be among the first cities, and the worn-out lands in that region of country, that are now owned in five hundred and one thousand acre tracts, (and hardly support a family at that,) would be divided into fifty acre tracts, each of which would be tilled by the hands of the hardy and intelligent republican, not only to yield a support, but competence and riches, to a large and happy family — happy in their industry and intelligence?

"No one dare deny that such would be the result. Is it not right, then, that we should express such opinions? We are parties interested as well as they; for what benefits or injures one part of the State, benefits or injures the other part."

A southern correspondent of the New York Observer thus expresses himself: "Though born and raised among the Green Mountains, I have been more than thirty years at the south, and I hold slaves; yet I think I can do justice to the feelings of north and south. I believe slavery is a curse to the south, and many others believe it, who will not own it, on account of the fanatic efforts of the abolitionists. When I speak of it as a curse, I mean in all its relations of master and servant — the bad influence it has upon our passions, upon our children, destroying that sense of moral responsibility which ought to bear upon us."

CHAPTER IX.

APPROACHES TO EMANCIPATION.

THE country found in its bosom, at the time of our confederation, about seven hundred thousand slaves. The following, from a recent number of the National Intelligencer, presents an accurate and clear view of an important part of our history in connection with this subject: —

THE CONSTITUTION AND SLAVERY. — The journal of the Convention to frame the present Constitution of the United States exhibits the following facts in connection with the subject of slavery: —

" The first committee on the subject consisted of Rutledge of South Carolina, Randolph of Virginia, Wilson of Pennsylvania, Gorham of Massachusetts, and Ellsworth of Connecticut; and they reported, as a section for the Constitution, 'that no tax or other duty should be laid on the migration or importation of such persons as the several States shall think proper to admit, nor shall such migration or importation *be prohibited.*' "

This was the first action of the Convention on the slavery question; and it will be seen that a committee, the majority of which were from what are strong antislavery States, reported against any future prohibition of the African slave trade, but were willing to legalize it perpetually.

This section was subsequently referred to a committee, selected by ballot, consisting of Langdon of New Hampshire, King of Massachusetts, Johnson of Connecticut, Livingston of New Jersey, Clymer of Pennsylvania, Dickinson of Delaware, Martin of Maryland, Madison of Virginia, Williamson of North Carolina, Pinckney of South Carolina, and Baldwin of Georgia.

This committee, a majority of which were from *slave States,* (then and now,) reported the clause, with authority to Congress to prohibit the slave trade after the year 1800, and in the mean time with authority to levy a tax on such importations. This section was afterwards modified and adopted as it now exists in the Constitution, extending the time before which Congress could not prohibit the trade until 1808 — Massachusetts, New Hampshire, and Connecticut, *free States,* and Maryland, North and South Carolina, slave States, voting for the extension; New Jersey and Pennsylvania, free States, and Delaware and Virginia, slave States, voting against it.

From the above it appears —

1. A committee, the majority of which were from *free States,* report in favor of denying to Congress the power at any period to prohibit the African slave trade.

2. That a subsequent *committee,* a majority of which were from the *slave States,* reported a new section, authorizing Congress to abolish the trade after the year 1800.

3. That this period was extended until the year 1808, thus giving eight additional years to the traffic, by the vote of New Hampshire, Massachusetts, and Connecticut, whilst the vote of Virginia was against such extension.

The New York Tribune, of about the same date, says, —

" Had the New England States voted against the extension, the slave trade would have been abolished eight years earlier, preventing the importation of more than a hundred thousand into this country, and there would have been at the present time a less number of slaves in the United States by at least three hundred thousand."

The southern heart and conscience at last found expression on the subject of Slavery in that most remarkable document adopted by the General Assembly of the

Presbyterian Church of the United States in 1818, and now contained in the Assembly's Digest. Its interest and its connection with what follows warrant its insertion here.

"The committee to which was referred the resolution on the subject of selling a slave, a member of the church, and which was directed to prepare a report to be adopted by the Assembly, expressing their opinion in general on the subject of slavery, reported, and, their report being read, was *unanimously* adopted, and referred to the same committee for publication. It is as follows, viz. : —

"The General Assembly of the Presbyterian Church, having taken into consideration the subject of SLAVERY, think proper to make known their sentiments upon it to the churches and people under their care.

"We consider the voluntary enslaving of one part of the human race by another as a gross violation of the most precious and sacred rights of human nature ; as utterly inconsistent with the law of God, which requires us to love our neighbor as ourselves ; and as totally irreconcilable with the spirit and principles of the gospel of Christ, which enjoin that 'all things whatsoever ye would that men should do to you, do ye even so to them.' Slavery creates a paradox in the moral system — it exhibits rational, accountable, and immortal beings in such circumstances as scarcely to leave them the power of moral action. It exhibits them as dependent on the will of others, whether they shall receive religious instruction ; whether they shall know and worship the true God ; whether they shall enjoy the ordinances of the gospel ; whether they shall perform the duties and cherish the endearments of husbands and wives, parents and children, neighbors and friends ; whether they shall preserve their chastity and purity, or regard the dictates of justice and humanity. Such are some of the consequences of slavery — consequences not imaginary — but which connect themselves with its very existence. The evils to which the slave is *always* exposed often take place in fact, and in their very worst degree and form ; and where all of them do not take place — as we rejoice to say that in many instances, through the influence of the principles of humanity and religion on the minds of masters, they do not, — still the slave is deprived of his natural right, degraded as a human being, and exposed to the danger of passing into the hands of a master who may inflict upon him all the hardships and injuries which inhumanity and avarice may suggest.

"From this view of the consequences resulting from the practice into which Christian people have most inconsistently fallen, of enslaving a portion of their *brethren* of mankind, — for 'God hath made of one blood all nations of men to dwell on the face of the earth,' — it is manifestly the duty of all Christians who enjoy the light of the present day, when the inconsistency of slavery, both with the dictates of humanity and religion, has been demonstrated, and is generally seen and acknowledged, to use their honest, earnest, and unwearied endeavors to correct the errors of former times, and as speedily as possible to efface this blot on our holy religion, and to obtain the complete abolition of slavery throughout Christendom, and if possible throughout the world.

"We rejoice that the church to which we belong commenced as early as any other in this country the good work of endeavoring to put an end to slavery, and that in the same work many of its members have ever since been, and now are, among the most active, vigorous, and efficient laborers. We do indeed tenderly sympathize with those portions of our church and our country where the evil of slavery has been entailed upon them; where a *great*, and *the most virtuous, part* of the *community* abhor slavery, and wish its extermination, as sincerely as any others, but where the number of slaves, their ignorance, and their vicious habits generally, render an immediate and universal emancipation inconsistent alike with the safety and happiness of the master and the slave. With those who are thus circumstanced we repeat that we tenderly sympathize. At the same time, we earnestly exhort them to continue, and, if possible, to increase their exertions to effect a total abolition of slavery. We exhort them to suffer no greater delay to take place in this most interesting concern than a regard to the public welfare *truly* and *indispensably* demands.

"As our country has inflicted a most grievous injury on the unhappy Africans, by bringing them into slavery, we cannot, indeed, urge that we should add a second injury to the first, by emancipating them in such a manner as that they will be likely to destroy themselves or others. But we do think that our country ought to be governed, in this matter, by no other consideration than an honest and impartial regard to the happiness of the injured party, uninfluenced by the expense or inconvenience which such a regard may involve. We therefore warn all who belong to our denomination of Christians against unduly extending this plea of necessity ; against making it a cover for the love and practice of slavery, or a pretence for not using efforts that are lawful and practicable to extinguish the evil.

" And we at the same time exhort others to forbear harsh censures and uncharitable reflections on their brethren, who unhappily live among slaves, whom they cannot immediately set free, but who, at the same time, are really using all their influence and all their endeavors to bring them into a state of freedom as soon as a door for it can be safely opened.

" Having thus expressed our views of slavery, and of the duty indispensably incumbent on all Christians to labor for its complete extinction, we proceed to recommend — and we do it with all the earnestness and solemnity which this momentous subject demands — a particular attention to the following points : —

" We recommend to all our people to patronize and encourage the Society, lately formed, for Colonizing in Africa, the land of their ancestors, the free people of color in our country. We hope that much good may result from the plans and efforts of this Society. And while we exceedingly rejoice to have witnessed its origin and organization among the *holders of slaves*, as giving an unequivocal pledge of their desire to deliver themselves and their country from the calamity of slavery, we hope that those portions of the American Union whose inhabitants are, by a gracious Providence, more favorably circumstanced, will cordially, and liberally, and earnestly coöperate with their brethren in bringing about the great end contemplated.

" We recommend to all the members of our religious denomination, not only to permit. but to facilitate and encourage, the instruction of their slaves in the principles and duties of the Christian religion ; by granting them liberty to attend on the preaching of the gospel, when they have the opportunity ; by favoring the instruction of them in Sabbath schools, wherever those schools can be formed ; and by giving them all other proper advantages for acquiring the knowledge of their duty both to God and man. We are perfectly satisfied, that as it is incumbent on all Christians to communicate religious instruction to those who are under their authority, so the doing of this in the case before us, so far from operating, as some have apprehended that it might, as an excitement to insubordination and insurrection, would, on the contrary, operate as the most powerful means for the prevention of those evils.

" We enjoin it on all church sessions and presbyteries, under the care of this Assembly, to discountenance, and, as far as possible, to prevent, all cruelty of whatever kind in the treatment of slaves ; especially the cruelty of separating husband and wife, parents and children ; and that which consists in selling slaves to those who will either themselves deprive these unhappy people of the blessings of the gospel, or who will transport them to places where the gospel is not proclaimed, or where it is forbidden to slaves to attend upon its institutions. The manifest violation or disregard of the injunction here given, in its true spirit and intention, ought to be considered as just ground for the discipline and censures of the church. And if it shall ever happen that a Christian professor, in our communion, shall sell a slave who is also in communion and good standing with our church, contrary to his or her will and inclination, it ought immediately to claim the particular attention of the proper church judicature ; and unless there be such peculiar circumstances attending the case as can but seldom happen, it ought to be followed, without delay, by a suspension of the offender from all the privileges of the church, till he repent, and make all the reparation in his power to the injured party."

Should the Old School General Assembly of the Presbyterian Church, embracing as it does most of the southern Presbyterian churches, adopt at their next annual meeting such an expression as this of their views in regard to slavery, would not the country feel that a vastly important step had been taken, if not toward the abolition of slavery, at least toward such an amelioration of it that it would soon cease to be an evil? What more would the north ask for the first step in that direction? Rather, would not a somewhat general apprehension be, that perhaps the Assembly had gone a little too far, and that greater caution, through fear of reaction, would have been advisable? What ecclesiastical body

at the north would or could now express a more decisive protest against the system? Every thing looked
like as speedy a removal of the evils of slavery as the
imperfection of human society and the slow processes
of reforming ancient customs allowed. This was not a
mere ecclesiastical movement, nor an impulse of right
feeling in the more zealous or fervent members of the
community. In Delaware, Maryland, Virginia, and
Kentucky, public sentiment warranted and sustained
this action. Jefferson's well-known protestations against
slavery were not the voice of one crying in a wilderness, but the exponent of extensive feeling on the
subject. Washington had said, " It is among my first
wishes to see some plan adopted by which slavery may
be abolished by law." Madison, a slaveholder, also said,
" It is wrong to admit into. the Constitution the idea of
property in man." After the ordinance of 1787 had
been passed, an interesting decision was made in Congress,
which was like a refusal to re-consider, and a re-affirma-
tion. Indiana, then a part of the North West Territory, petitioned Congress for leave to hold slaves for a
certain term. A committee, of which a southern slaveholder was chairman, reported against it, and the petition was rejected.*

A great change very soon came over the south. Remonstrances from among themselves, legislative measures, free, earnest discussions of slavery, all tending to
its removal as soon as the best method could be determined, were suddenly hushed.

This phenomenon is strangely accounted for, on the
part of many at the north, by saying that about this

* Oration, July 4, 1854, by T. K. King, Esq., Providence, R. I.

time the cotton interest assumed very great importance, and the antislavery feeling at the south was therefore suppressed.

He who believes this, makes an imputation which hardly does credit to his knowledge of human nature; it certainly reflects too much upon the Christian character of a community distinguished for intellectual and moral excellence. The names of some who were foremost at that day in guiding public sentiment sufficiently refute this suspicion. Neither can it be shown that there were at that time those astounding revelations of the profitableness of cotton as would suggest the probability of so great a change of views and feelings with regard to a moral question; and as such, slavery specially presented itself.

The manner in which this change of feeling and action is now universally accounted for at the south suggests the more probable explanation.

About that time people at the north were seized with deep convictions that American slavery was a system of iniquity, and should forthwith be abolished; that it was a sin *per se* to hold a fellow-being in bondage; and that all sin should be immediately repented of and forsaken. Accordingly abolition societies were formed to effect the immediate emancipation of the slaves. Publications were scattered through the south whose direct tendency was to stir up insurrection among the colored people.

A traveling agent of a northern society was arrested, and, on searching his trunk, there were found some prints, which might well have wrought, as they did, upon the feelings of the southern people. These prints were pictorial illustrations of the natural equality before God of all men, without distinction of color, and setting forth the happy fruits of a universal acknowledgment of this truth, by exhibiting a white woman in no equivocal relations to a colored man. Incendiary sentiments and pictures had for some time made their appearance on northern handkerchiefs, for southern children and servants. The old-fashioned, blue-paper wrappers of chocolate had within them some eminently suggestive emblems. When these amalgamation pictures were discovered, husbands and fathers at the south considered that whatever might be true of slavery ·as a system, self-defence, the protection of their households against a servile insurrection, was their first duty. Who can wonder that they broke into the post-office, and seized and burned abolition papers; indeed, no excesses are surprising, in view of the perils to which they saw themselves exposed. Then ensued those more stringent laws, so general now throughout the slaveholding States, forbidding the slaves to be publicly instructed. Those laws remain to the present day; they are disregarded, indeed, to a very great extent, by the people themselves; but they remain in order to be enforced against northern interference.

Yet the paralyzing influence of the causes which led to such legislation continues. We wonder at it, and so do our southern friends. To the question why various things are not done to improve the condition of the blacks, the perpetual answer from men and women who seek no apology for indolence or cupidity is, "We are afraid of your abolitionists. Whoever moves for redress in any of these things is warned that he is playing into the hands of northern fanatics." They seem to be living in a state of self-defence, of self-preservation, against the north.

The following communications to the New York Observer contain valuable information: —

JEFFERSON CO., VA., February 13.

Messrs. Editors : In answer to your request that some of your readers acquainted with the laws of Virginia would send you the truth of the matter relating to the teaching of slaves, I have referred to the Virginia code. In chapter 198, entitled, Of Offences against Public Policy, section 31 provides, — every *assemblage of negroes,* "for the purpose of instruction in reading and writing, or in the nighttime for any purpose, shall be an unlawful assembly." "Any justice may issue his warrant to any officer, or to any other person, requiring him to enter any place where such *assemblage* may be, and seize any negro therein ; and he, or any other justice, may order any such negro to be punished with stripes."

Section 32 is as follows : " If a white person *assemble* with negroes for the purpose of instructing them to read or write, or if he associates with them in an *unlawful assembly,* he shall be confined in jail not exceeding six months, and fined not exceeding one hundred dollars ; and any justice may require him to enter into a recognizance, with sufficient security, to appear before the Circuit, County, or Corporation Court, of the county or corporation where the offence was committed, to answer therefor, and in the mean time to keep the peace and be of his good behavior."

You will perceive that by the terms of this law a master or mistress is not forbidden to teach his or her own servants to read. Such, I believe, is the general understanding in the State ; and it often happens that the young members of the family do teach the negroes in the family to read.

This law was first passed in 1830 or 1831.

A VIRGINIA LAWYER.

Messrs. Editors: In your paper of the 9th, information is asked from some one "acquainted with the laws of Virginia" on the subject of " *teaching slaves.*" I can furnish it in the simple recital of a historical fact.

About five years ago, Dr. E., of A—— county, died, leaving, by will, all his slaves, some thirty-four in number, free, and appropriated fifty thousand dollars in bonds, well secured, for their personal benefit. They were to be kept on the plantation for five years, to be educated and prepared for freedom under the control and direction of the nephew of the testator, who was the executor of the will and residuary legatee. As agent of the Colonization Society, the subject came under my cognizance. The nephew was anxious to fulfill the important trust committed to him, and proposed to petition the legislature to allow him to educate the slaves in letters. This led me to a personal and thorough investigation of the subject. I then learned from the highest authority, legal and political, that the statute on the subject allowed owners to teach their slaves *in their own families,* but not to employ a schoolmaster for this purpose. Thus the law, somewhat equivocal in terms, has always been construed. The object of the law was not designed to control the liberality of the master in the matter, but to protect the country against a foreign influence by excluding irresponsible teachers.

History contains few plots more appalling than some which were detected among the slaves just on the eve of being carried into effect. As northern zeal has promulgated bolder sentiments with regard to the right and duty of slaves to steal, burn, and kill, in effecting their liberty, the south has intrenched itself by more vigorous laws and customs; and it is not strange that in argument also some positions should be taken which once would have found no defenders. Nothing forces itself more constantly upon the thoughts of a northerner at the south, who looks into the history and present state of slavery, than the vast injury which has resulted from northern interference. We sometimes speak of the black man, in his relation to the human family, as " Joseph," whom his brethren have sold into slavery. If the black man at the south is "Joseph," there are those at the north, who, with less violence to truth than to rhetorical correctness, may be called " Potiphar's wife," by whom "Joseph" has been put into deeper bondage; " whose feet they hurt with fetters; he was laid in irons." A pastor of a large colored church at the south writes to me, "Many of the higher class of citizens sustain me in my labors by their approval; but many cherish, I fear, a latent suspicion of abolition, insurrection, &c. Meanwhile, I strive simply to preach Christ crucified."

There are men at the south who maintain that so long as the existence of society there depends upon the subjection of the colored to the white race, it is better for the blacks to depend wholly on oral instruction. Taught to read, it is said, they will be unfitted for their servile condition, through the information which they will in many ways acquire. It has been said, for substance, by high authority, in the debates of a State convention at the south, "To make the slaves most useful to us, and most contented and happy, we must shut up some of the avenues by which knowledge would reach their minds. They can be taught orally every thing essential to salvation; they can thus be made familiar with the word of God; they can be intelligent Christians, as we see many of them are, without reading." Those who say this will tell you that their philanthropy in this thing is wiser and better than yours, and that, after all, they give their slaves more instruction than white servants receive.

Though this is not the common sentiment, it is nevertheless fortified and defended by appeals made to the principles of self-preservation in southern citizens against the north. Were there entire kindness and confidence between the north and south on the subject of slavery, any attempt to shut up the Bible from the most unrestricted use by the slaves would be overborne by Christian benevolence. Nothing could prevent the slaves from being as generally instructed as the whites are where common schools do not prevail; and where they do prevail, the slaves would indirectly partake of these benefits. But if one thing is more obvious than another to a friendly northerner at the south, it is that northern interference is largely responsible for withholding the Word of God from the hands of millions of souls in our land. A common and favorite name of some at the north, who are extremely and conscientiously interested in the abolition of slavery, is, "friends of the slave." It would make some of them weep to see what a practical misnomer this is.

Invariably, the answer to every question about teaching the slaves to read, from men who were not capable of excusing themselves from Christian duty, was, "If you will give us a chance to do something besides defending ourselves against northern agitators, we will satisfy every reasonable expectation on those points. While we are cursed, and threatened, and ecclesiastical bodies are making presentments of us before Heaven, and invoking divine vengeance upon us, and foreign people are stirred up against us, and we are irritated by having our colored people decoyed from us, and we know not who are lurking among us to excite insurrections, how can we be expected to make progress in reformations? Grant that it is our plain duty to instruct the slaves in reading the Word of God in defiance of all danger. It is not in human nature to do its duty under compulsion from equals. When you say to a man, 'You shall,' human nature says, 'I won't,' however just your demand may be. We at the south are no better naturally than you, and you would do as we do, if you were treated like us."

Bad men at the south are furnished by some forms of northern agitation, not only with excuses for their consciences, but with the short logic of retaliation, to justify the hardships in slavery; and there are enough of such men every where, loud and denunciatory, to exert great control in popular assemblies, where Christian meekness can not make its voice heard. Good men every where are apt to give way before the furious blasts of passion which come from such a quarter; and though they mourn over it, they say it is useless to resist, for such men get the popular ear, and stir up popular feeling against a good measure. Conservative men, even when in the majority, are disposed to yield when conscientious radicals oppose them; and they submit to defeat by such men with a good grace, while radicals are apt to be factious and rebellious if they can not have their own way. When a strong movement was made in one of the legislatures at the south to raise the term of years within which a child should not be sold, something was indeed gained; but one argument against the whole proposition was, " It is a concession to the abolitionists." The gentleman who drafted the act told me that the proposition to forbid the sale of a child under twelve or thirteen years of age was voted down under the influence of appeals and warnings, strange as they seem to us, against northern exultations.   Now, a child five years old may, in that State, be sold and removed from its parents. We are verily guilty concerning our brother. Wisdom and kindness in a private individual lead him to refrain from exasperating even the unreasonable feelings of one who is believed to be in error; to cease from aggravating prejudice and passion is commonly regarded as the most effectual way to promote a desirable object. This has not characterized our treatment of slavery and the south. Up to the present moment outrages are committed in the name of freedom and humanity, which must result, if not checked, in a state of things which it is sad to contemplate. What community can long endure such assaults as these without resorting to retaliatory measures leading to scenes of personal and sectional contest? Late papers tell us that, within a few weeks, —

"A slave girl was taken from a railroad train at Salem, Columbiana county, Ohio, by force. She clung to her mistress, but was carried off by a large negro, who flourished a pistol amidst the applause of the spectators. Her master offered to go before an officer with her and execute free papers, leaving the girl to remain free or to go forth with him; but the mob would not suffer it."

CHAPTER X.

WHAT SHALL WE DO?

WE have been most singularly foiled in our plans and purposes with regard to the removal of slavery from this country, and more recently with regard to its extension beyond its old dominion. We have legislated and protested, prayed and preached, against the extension of slavery, and this day it is more than ever lengthening its cords and strengthening its stakes.

We have done that which we supposed to be our duty. We have walked according to the best light that we could obtain. We have become educated to a more intense interest in the black man than in all the other races together; and perhaps it is because God intends that we should have more to do on this continent with him than with any other race.

What strange adversity has followed those who have been foremost in the antislavery cause! The south was just on the eve of abolishing slavery; the abolitionists arose, and put it back within its innermost intrenchments. We had succeeded, as we thought, in restricting slavery to its ancient limits, when the liberty party, by their well-known decisive influence in a presidential election, added that vast State of Texas to slave territory.

By our antislavery agitation and its influence on the south, as we are told, she has simply acted in self-defence and has just succeeded in getting permission for slavery to extend itself into the new regions of our country.

What is to be the end of this contest? What shall we do?

SECTION I. — *Dissolution of the Union an Absurdity.*

" Let us peaceably dissolve the Union," is one answer. " Let us make a partition of our whole territory, and let slavery have undisturbed possession of its separate domain."

A peaceable separation of the Union is an impossibility. Peace at the separation, or afterwards, will be looked for in vain. A peaceable dissolution of our planetary system might almost as well be expected.

But allowing it to be possible, some thoughts and questions naturally arise at such a proposition.

Would slavery be diminished by this movement? Would the wrongs and woes of the black man be lessened? Clearly not, as a necessary result.

" But we should wash our hands from all participation in them."

This end of responsibility would no doubt be a sublime spectacle to some; but there is an undefined and unsuspected step connected with every thing sublime, which sometimes lands the actor at the foot of all his greatness.

If men's consciences and sensibilities are now disturbed so much at the "enormous wrongs of slavery," how would it be if tales of perpetual woe should reach them from that future prison ship, the southern confederacy, with its growing millions of slaves confined beneath the hatches? If the slave trade has moved civilized nations to arm themselves against it, could our northern philanthropists be quiet with a land of slavery festering, as they would suppose, with pollution and guilt?

Suppose that the slave trade should be revived by the south, at least through privateers from the south and north. War would then cover the seas; commerce would faint and fail. Fugitive slaves would be demanded at the point of the bayonet, and armies would meet armies.

The south, perhaps, would enter into a commercial treaty with Great Britain. Canada would then be closed, if not before, against fugitive slaves. The south would have its own tariff and ships. Our ship builders would go where their business led them; cotton would no less rule the world than now. A great impulse would be given to the planting interest. Manufactures go with commerce. The north would pay a good price for her virtuous abhorrence of evil, and look like a ghostly anchorite, while British capitalists, descendants of Clarkson and Wilberforce, (such is human nature,) would no doubt profit by our dissolution of partnership.

This is one picture. Another is this. The Christian men and women at the south, relieved of all interference from the north, would begin the work of reforming every evil among them incident to slavery. Treaties with Great Britain would prevent slaves from fleeing to Canada, and the free States would reject them. The partition of the Union would give the south more territory to be an outlet for their surplus black population. Laws would be passed more humane to the slave than we ever dreamed of, and a great and flourishing community of Christianized black people would cover the slaveholding

States. The American Colonization Society — the child
of the south — would receive multitudes of emancipated
negroes to Christianize and colonize Africa. Such have
been the marvelous acts of divine grace to the Africans,
in bringing them, through the cupidity and sinfulness of
men, to this country, and saving a great multitude of
them, that it requires neither strong faith nor fancy to
suppose that this work might still go on, in the form of
interchange of the blacks between Africa and the Southern States. The south has learned to be, and is fitted
to be, the protector and friend of the African. The
proportion of cruelty and wickedness due to human nature every where has been, of course, enacted there;
but God is there, and his gospel, and his Spirit, and his
elect; and as sure as Christ is to reign through the earth,
the Christians at the south will vindicate themselves as
the benefactors of the colored race. A great amount of
influence at the south is ready to assert its power in this
direction as soon as the necessity of self-defence is taken
away by the restoration of sympathy and kindness on
our part. Far better than to rend this Union into two
hostile republics, or to let the south, by separating ourselves from her, accomplish by herself what might be
her destined ministry toward the colored race, there is a
way of peaceful agreement and of union to do an im-
mense amount of good to the colored people, which we
may reach if God will but hold us back awhile from
our precipitancy.

We had in 1850 three millions two hundred and four
thousand three hundred and thirteen slaves in the United
States, and in 1860 we shall have not far from nine hundred thousand more ; for their increase for the last ten
years was at the rate of twenty-eight and eight tenths

per centum. They cannot be emancipated to remain here. It would be to their misery and destruction.

SECTION II. — *Results to be expected from Emancipation.*

The conviction forced itself upon my mind at the south, that the most disastrous event to the colored people would be their emancipation to live on the same soil with the whites.

The two distinct races could not live together except by the entire subordination of one to the other. Protection is now extended to the blacks; their interests are the interests of the owners. But ceasing to be a protected class, they would fall a prey to avarice, suffer oppression and grievous wrongs, encounter the rivalry of white immigrants, which is an element in the question of emancipation here, and nowhere else. Antipathy to their color would not diminish, and being the feebler race, they would be subjected to great miseries.

All history shows that two races of men approaching in any considerable degree to equality in numbers can not live together unless intermarriages take place.* The Sabine women prepared the way for the admission of the Sabines to Rome, and gave them a place among the conscript fathers. Alexander, having conquered Persia, married the Persian Roxana, and thus lessened the social distance between the new provinces and the original empire. Alaric, Clovis, Henry I. of England, in Italy, Gaul, and among the Saxons, respectively, resorted to the same policy of intermarriage

* Carey's Domestic Slavery.

for the same purpose. The long dissensions between the Normans and Saxons under William Duke of Normandy and William Rufus disappeared when the two races followed the example of Henry. We know the happy results.

On the other hand, Egypt and Israel, the Hebrew people and the nations conquered by them, the Spaniards and Moors, many modern nations and the Jews, prove the impossibility of two races living together unless one race is dependent, or they intermarry. Like the Moors and the Jews, the blacks would eventually be driven out. Even now, in some places at the south the free blacks are prohibited by the laws of certain crafts, the stone cutter's for example, from lifting a tool in their work. White servants are exclusively employed in one of the largest hotels at the south.

The fighting propensity of the lower class of the Irish would expose the blacks to constant broils through the rivalry of labor. The following is a specimen: —

IRISH AND NEGRO ROW IN BUFFALO. — There was a protracted and somewhat bloody fight yesterday afternoon, on the dock at the foot of Washington Street, between some negroes and Irishmen. The parties were about equal in point of numbers when the affair began ; but the Irish soon collected in great force, and considering it a free fight, counted themselves in, until poor Cuffee had not a ghost of a chance. Three of the negroes were badly beaten, one of them to such an extent that it was supposed he must die; but he is better this morning, and will probably recover. Some six or eight of the combatants, black and white, were before the justice this morning, with a large number of witnesses to complicate the investigation. It seems to have been a sort of spontaneous outbreak, without any other cause than the mutual jealousy and dislike subsisting between the Celtic and African races. Before the police were able to suppress the row, something like a thousand persons had collected, besides those directly engaged in the affray. — *Buffalo Advertiser, June 5*, 1854.

It would not be strange if, as the least evil, and to prevent their being exterminated, or driven out, as John Randolph's emancipated slaves and other companies of emancipated negroes have been, by one free State after another, or leading a wretched life like that of our New England Indians, it should be considered best for all concerned that they should enter again, after being emancipated, into some form of subordination to the whites. Their present bondage, with all its evils, real or supposed, it would then be seen, is by no means the worst condition into which they could fall.

Their women would be debased without measure if set free. So far from being surprised at any degree of looseness in morals among the slaves, one can only feel grateful for the influences of religion and so much of public sentiment as prevail among them to keep so large a proportion of them virtuous, as, considering their temperament and their place in society, it is believed exists. But let them be thrown wholly upon their own resources for subsistence, or subjected to the idle life which they would be tempted to lead, and the probable consequence to the blacks and whites, and to their posterity, would be fearful.

As an ardent friend of the colored race, I am compelled to believe that while they remain with us, subordination in some form to a stronger race is absolutely necessary for their protection and best welfare — a subordination, however, which shall be for the interests of the black man, as well as for his superiors, and from which every degree of oppression shall be purged away, the idea of their being doomed as a race or caste being abolished, and individual tendencies and aptitudes being regarded. If our southern brethren will protect and provide for them for this world and the next, we, as friends of man, should feel that we owe them a debt of gratitude and should be willing to assist, if necessary, in promoting their welfare.

Suppose, then, that we begin to take some new view of our duty with regard to slavery, having long enough, and uselessly, and injuriously enough beleaguered and battered it, only to find, in 1854, that, in spite of all our efforts and prayers, it is taking a stride more vast and astonishing than ever. A physician who had failed in his course of treatment, as we have with slavery, would ordinarily change it. Perhaps we are wrong. If our aim is good, perhaps we can effect it in a better way — a way in which the south itself will coöperate with us. Perhaps this whole continent can be pacified on this subject consistently with truth and right-eousness, and to the increased happiness of all con-cerned.

SECTION III. — *Social Divisions deplored.*

May we see the day when, like mercy and truth, the north and south shall meet together, and righteousness and peace shall kiss each other. There is real respect for the north, and attachment to it, on the part of the south, when they are not reminded of differences of opinion about slavery. They earnestly covet our advantages of education for their children, whom they would be glad to send here during some portion of their school days; but non-intercourse, except for purposes of trade, greatly prevails. Teachers from the north are sometimes subject to the jealousies and un-kindness of those who, having no personal interest in their object as teachers, look upon them as spies, and deprecate the influence over young persons and servants which the natural repugnance of these northern teachers to slavery may silently exert.

The privileges of our sea-shore retreats, so highly prized by southerners, are not enjoyed by them as formerly. There are cases of real suffering in which many people at the south feel themselves debarred from our northern means of health and comfort.

How sad it made me feel to see the great Baptist communion in our country divided by this slavery question; and when my soul was melted by the eloquence of Methodist brethren preaching Jesus to the slaves, it was painful to think that the same ploughshare had furrowed a deep line of separation between them and their northern friends; nor could I without sorrow hear members of those Presbyterian churches of the south, which still prefer to coöperate with the American Board of missions, lament that the Board can not consistently send its agents into slave States to foster the spirit of missions. O thou enemy of God and man, what joy must it be to thee in this way, and by this means, to have rent asunder God's elect, preventing them, too, from affectionate counsel and effort for the good of the African.

What communion we used to have with southern friends here! But now they feel and act as though accused of crime. Indeed every where in the south, where you get access to the hearts of the people, there is something like the sorrowful moaning of the sea, as though there had been, or would yet be, a great tempest.

I felt that we had not treated the south as we would desire to be treated — as human nature requires to be treated; that we had not spoken to her, or dealt with her, as we ought to have done.

On what subject, except slavery, has the south ever divided from the north, in Congress or out of Congress, in war or peace?

What pride we have had in her patriots, statesmen, and scholars, and what fellowship with her sainted dead!

What a goodly land she possesses; what historical associations belong to her; what resources of wealth are there; what renown by sea and land; in cabinets, at home and abroad!

If the south should by any means obtain and keep the ascendency in our national councils, in what way would she have the power and disposition to conflict with northern interests, leaving the subject of slavery and our sensibilities out of the question?

With regard to what are called the encroachments of the slave power, the demands of the south, are they at all to our injury except as they offend our opinions and feelings on the subject of slavery? Political appointments would be made with less of a sectional spirit if we were at peace.

One would think that the south were Philip of Macedon, and we at the north the states of Greece, judging from our philippics against her. But her great offence is, independently of every thing else, the perpetuation of an evil under which both of us were born, but which we at the north were enabled to remove; an effort on the part of the south to defend and maintain her institution of slavery under the constitution: to maintain the right guarantied by our social compact, but assailed by us. We seem to have forgotten how the royal family of the mother country, the king and queen at the head, and many of the nobles, contributed toward the first

importation of slaves from Africa to this country; how
Jefferson in his first draught of the Declaration of Independence, charges the king with making depredations
on an innocent people, and inflicting them as slaves on
us; and how, at the close of the war, we at the north
lengthened out the importation of slaves to the south
beyond the term voted for by a majority of the Southern
States. Nor do we consider that the south was approx-
imating the work of emancipation by public discussions,
by acts of assembly drawn up and ready to be proposed,
and by votes in her ecclesiastical bodies, when the outbreak of northern o¨ ¨osition to slavery, and attempts to
emancipate the slaves at once, drove back the south
from her purpose, and that all her subsequent attempts
at the extension of slavery have been intended as retaliatory acts, or in self-defence.

This is true up to the time of the Nebraska bill and
the repeal of the Missouri compromise, measures capable of no defence. The hitherto indomitable attachments of party are yielding to the stronger, the uncor-
rupted sense of violated truth. The accumulating force
of public opinion is sweeping down upon all who dare
defend that disregard of those principles which every
man needs for his protection.

It is not yet time, but the day may not be distant,
when, with sorrow over our vanquished opponent in this
Nebraska measure, we shall begin to think whether we
have not extended our retaliatory feelings too indiscrim-
inately against southern men. For, after all, the people at the south generally took but little interest in the
Nebraska measure. I was in South Carolina when the
news of the passage of the Nebraska bill arrived; and
it was received with almost no sensation, except where

the struggle had been watched, and there the decision
of course brought relief. But a very frequent expression was, ' It is a great pity that our politicians should
have stirred up this strife; we were doing very well
before; it will make trouble for us, and we shall gain
nothing.' It deserves to be considered that politicians
at the south lead the people far more than with us. We
have more popular assemblages; public opinion is ascer-
tained more readily, and is brought to bear more forcibly upon public men here. Besides, at the south, the
towering names and influence of a long succession of accomplished statesmen have given the people more of ac-
quiescence in their political leaders. Immigration and
the general weakening of all political relationships are
every where effecting a change in this respect. But
should we punish the south for the acts of her politicians,
for which, indeed, she must be held responsible, the people generally would not be conscious of having done any
thing to deserve chastisement.

Then with regard to some of those who at home ad-
vocated the measure. While we look at it as extending
a great curse over a territory dedicated to freedom, some
of them, who are not influenced by political considerations, take no such view of slavery, but think of a planter removing to Nebraska with slaves, as of a Massachusetts man removing to Rhode Island with his apprentices. This does not extenuate their disregard of our
feelings and opinions, but may serve to lower the tone
of our retaliation as against the whole southern people.

This breach of national faith is so remarkable that it
places itself among those convulsions in the moral world
which under God have prepared the way for great de-
velopments in the destiny of a people. What good will

ever result from it, or what its evil consequences may be, human foresight cannot discover. If some great development of Providence with regard to the African race in connection with the American people were approaching, we should connect the two things in our thoughts, and wait for the result. Let us think of this. We look at the Africans only as slaves; God looks at them as immortal beings. We legislate about them as a basis of representation; God plans for them as subjects of redeeming love. Our thoughts are absorbed by their sufferings in slavery; God contemplates them in a worse bondage, and would bring them into his family. If he has any further designs for the good of their race by our means, this beginning of a revelation, this opening of a seal, has taken place with as little violence, as, under the circumstances, we could have expected.

Fraudulent as we declare the Nebraska measure to have been, yet considering the violent opposition to the fugitive slave law at the north, we can not wonder that southern politicians caught at it, when offered to them by northern men, as affording a defence to slavery at home against the north. What had the south done to injure us, except through our sensibilities on the subject of slavery? What have we done to her, but admonish, threaten, and indict her before God, excommunicate her, stir up insurrection among her slaves, endanger her homes, make her Christians and ministers odious in other lands? And now that she has availed herself of a northern measure for her defence, we are ready to move the country from its foundations. We ought to reflect, whether we have not been enforcing our moral sentiments upon the south in offensive ways, so as to constitute that oppression which makes even a wise man mad.

All this time we have overlooked the intrinsic difficulties of the evil which the south has had to contend with; have disagreed among ourselves about sin *per se*, and about the question of immediate or gradual emancipation, and yet have expected the south to be clear on these points, and to act promptly. Previous to her recent conduct, instead of being more passionate and revengeful under such treatment, it is rather to be wondered at that the south had conducted herself so well. What had she ever done, except in self-defence, in our long quarrel, which, upon reconciliation, would rankle in our memories, and make it hard for us to forgive and forget? Positively, not one thing. We have been the assailants, she the mark; we the prosecutors, she the defendant; we the accusers, she the self-justifying respondent.

Unless we choose to live in a state of perpetual war, we must prevent and punish all attempts to decoy slaves from their masters. Whatever our repugnance to slavery may be, there is a law of the land, a Constitution, to which we must submit, or employ suitable means to change it. While it remains, all our appeals to a "higher law" are fanaticism.

SECTION IV. — *Return to the Constitution.*

We must return to that simple provision in that Constitution which cemented our confederation. We must do this, or break up the compact. If enactments are necessary to enforce this provision, they must not trench upon other rights. They must especially guard every free man from having his liberty put in peril. The common gratuity of justice to every accused person — presumption of innocence — must be extended to the colored man under arrest. We must review our doings on this subject, and come to an agreement, by which the provisions of the Constitution shall be enforced with the least possible ground of objection. The north will never rest till some obnoxious features in the present fugitive slave law are changed.

We are liable to imposition from colored men through strong sympathy for fugitive slaves. Cases are known in which the same set of papers has been used by different colored men to collect money. In a city of Massachusetts, there were not long since, and probably are now, several hundred dollars, which a colored man, pretending to be a fugitive slave, had collected; but being exposed, he has since been afraid to appear and claim the money, though he has employed various means to come into possession of it.

We must not think that every fugitive slave is necessarily and properly the object of compassion, to be cherished and caressed; that his master is a proper object of aversion. Some at the north have sympathized with a fictitious being in the person of a fugitive slave. I will relate a case of deep interest, well known at the south, and representing other cases which in our zeal we overlook.

A slave came to the door of a rich gentleman, an excellent man, in a southern city, representing that, being in feeble health and unable therefore to do his master's work, he had obtained leave from his master to become this gentleman's servant if he would buy him. The gentleman did not need him, but, from compassion, bought him, and favored him in his labor. Some time after, on going with his family to the north, he took this slave with him, chiefly because it would be for his health.

While at the north, the servant came to him, and asked for money to buy some articles for his wife at home. He received some money, and that night deserted his master, and was brought before the court to have his freedom effected by his friends.

The master stated to the court that the servant was of hardly any value to him; at present he was an expence and burden; and that he was perfectly willing to abandon him, though he expressed his opinion of such conduct on the part of the slave, and his apprehension that freedom would not prove to be his greatest blessing. He obtained his freedom.

Had that slave fled to my house for refuge the evening that he left his master, and had I known all the circumstances of his case, would I have done well to harbor or countenance him?

"Certainly," replies one; "to be owned as property by a fellow-being is a greater wrong than any theft, ingratitude, or unkindness, of which he may be guilty. I would deliver him from bondage, then reprove him, and let him suffer for his wrong doing."

But for the conclusion of the story. When the master was returning to the south, the weak, sickly man came to him, and besought him to take him back. He protested that he had had enough of freedom, that he had been imposed upon by his friends, and that he should be miserable to be left behind.

Should his master have yielded to his request? "No," says one; "he had no right to own a fellow-being as a slave; not even to support him without any remuneration, or to nurse him in sickness, or to pension him for life from his estate. Better, far better, to do right than to do kindly. *Fiat justitia ruat cœlum.*"

The master at first declined to receive him, but finally referred him to the ladies of the family, through whose influence he obtained leave to go back. He was, however, told by his master to return to his "friends," and consult with them, and, if he concluded to go back to the south, to be on board the steamer by a certain hour. Early the next morning he secretly hired a carriage and went on board, and is now at the south.

All that I saw and heard has brought me to this conclusion — that, in aiding a fugitive slave on his way to Canada, if at all, I must know whom I am helping, and for what reasons he has fled. I do not feel as I once did, that his fleeing from slavery is presumptive evidence that he ought to be assisted to escape. On his arrest he ought to be presumed to be free till he is proved to be a slave. We must insist on this; we have free colored citizens who otherwise may be kidnapped; but a fugitive slave may owe service to one who has redeemed him, at his own request, from a bad master, or in other ways laid himself under obligations, which he violates in fleeing, as much as any fugitive debtor. A fugitive slave is not necessarily, nor as a matter of course, an object of compassion; it is not certain that he has fled from a bad to a better condition; that freedom in Boston is invariably preferable to slavery in Charleston.

We of the free States are too apt to invest a slave, especially a fugitive, with an interest which may be overwrought; to our eye he is the incarnation of injured innocence; liberty, priceless liberty, is personated in him; to have fled from a master at the south is incontestable evidence, in our eyes, that he is a true man, contending for Heaven's boon, freedom, and in his proportion he seems worthy of a place with patriots.

All this seems humane and philanthropic; it reads well; in a speech it brings applause, in a sermon tears; but now and then it is likely to be misplaced philanthropy, the sheerest of romancing, and practically great unkindness to its object. There are colored men and women at the north and west who have fled from brutal treatment, such as would make any human being risk death in any shape to escape from it. Masters acknowledge this, and men who are guilty of the treatment referred to are as much detested and avoided at the south as the bad members of any craft with us are by their fellows. Should a fugitive bring me proof that he was fleeing from certain planters whom I could name, my instinctive feeling would be the same as in pulling a shipmate away from a shark. Southerners would feel in the same way. No rule was ever made that could determine a man's duty in such cases. If we go to the Bible, we find, on the one hand, Hagar, sent back, not to Abraham, but to Sarai, her mistress, who had "dealt hardly with her;" and she is told to "submit" herself "under her hands." Again: the Apostles are repeatedly set free from prison by divine interposition. Socrates refuses an opportunity to escape, and gives his reasons for remaining in prison and drinking the hemlock; while a hundred cases in which good men have acted otherwise are not condemned by the voice of mankind. We can not settle questions on this subject by a rule any more than we can give a rule for revolutions. There are some things, however, pertaining to this subject, which are clear. Our error at the north is in supposing that every fugitive must be presumed to be worthy of aid in effecting his escape. Romantic adventures, by women as well as men, in secreting and sending away safely a fugitive slave sometimes have the thrilling interest of the rescue of a child from a burning house, or from the waves; when, perhaps, great injustice and unkindness have been perpetrated. Some children escaping from parents, some wives from husbands, would properly be protected and aided, the world over; but we may as justly aid in every case of elopement, or get a voyage for every runaway boy, as help every fugitive slave. If called upon by a sheriff to aid in capturing a fugitive of any description, I have a right to decide whether I will not refuse, and abide the penalty of a refusal.

Every man can abate a nuisance without waiting for a process of law; but he must convince the court that it was a nuisance which would not admit of delay. If he proves this, he is justified. On this principle we may help any fugitive slave; but we are held to answer before a higher law than that of man whether the circumstances justified us in setting aside or resisting the laws of the land. If not, though we may escape in human courts, our sin against God, through his ordinance of government, remains.

After we have said and done all which it is possible for human wisdom to do in making the recovery of slaves inoffensive, as things now are, there will remain in many the deep sectional difference of inborn feelings with regard to the whole subject; and it can never cease, as now viewed by both sides, from being a source of disquietude, resulting in alienations and unnumbered private and public evils, unless we all agree to abide faithfully by the Constitution until it is changed. It offends our moral sense, we will suppose, to have a man who has tried to escape and be free, taken back to involuntary servitude. But there are other interests for moral sense to be concerned about besides those of a fugitive black man. Until we are separated from the south by dividing the Union, while we live under our present Constitution, our moral sense must be more intelligent and comprehensive. We may well be reminded that moral sense agreed in 1787, for the sake of certain objects which could not otherwise be accomplished, to suffer in silence, and let persons held to service and escaping be recovered. Now, to rouse ourselves up, and say it shall not be done, is treacherous. We have obtained the benefits of constitutional government ; and shall we now repudiate the compromise by which they were gained? We may use all proper means to have slavery abolished; but while it remains as it now is, we must submit to the recovery of fugitive slaves, or to anarchy, or to dissolution of the Union. All appeals to our feelings, on this subject, when the case of a fugitive slave is pending, are as really out of place, if the object be to hinder the process of law, as appeals against a sheriff's doings in attaching and selling private property.

Can any one inform us where northern moral sense was, or whether it was in the convention when the north protracted the slave trade eight years longer than the south wished to endure it? If in the convention, it must have had leave of absence when the vote on that measure was taken. It is now very clamorous in every debate on slavery, and it ought to be called to order, being reminded that its silence or consent in 1787, works a forfeiture of all right of remonstrance now, at least till it has raised money enough to pay for three hundred thousand slaves which are here in consequence of those eight years during which the slave trade was continued by northern votes.

When a slave has fled, and established himself in business here, and a family is rising around him, an attempt to force him back to slavery does violence to the feelings of every citizen. If a statute of limitations with regard to debts, libels, land titles, and other things, is founded on natural principles of justice, we may expect that when a better state of feeling exists between the north and south, we shall obtain a statute of limitations with regard to the recovery of slaves. Until that time, cases of a trying nature must be provided for in an amicable manner. It is easy to clamor about such cases, but it is wiser to treat them as we do other trials; and these certainly are among the afflictions which are not relieved by violence.

A distinguished advocate, defending a fugitive slave before a court, urged this as a reason why the slave should not be given up — that he might be, or would be, sold by his master as soon as he should arrive in a southern State.

This would be a proper and commendable motive in defending one not yet proved to be a slave; but if urged as a reason why the slave, being proved such, should not be delivered to his master, it expresses, with all its kindness and tenderness, the principle of mob law. Soft and gentle, like thistle down it has a seed of evil for its centre. What though the probability were that the slave would be sold at auction as soon as he could be taken over the boundary line of a slave State ? The Constitution of the United States must not be nullified in its fugitive slave provision for that reason, unless we seek to make a revolution. We must go to work in another way to make things accord with our sense of justice; and if that way be slow, it is the only way to prevent still greater evils. Until we divide the Union, or procure a change in the Constitution, if we resist one of its provisions from repugnance to it, and so nullify it, we make a breach in a dam which has behind it a desolating river. That lawyers should do or counsel this, not from professional necessity, but moved by their sensibilities, fills even some clergymen with surprise. Our clerical calling cherishes our sensibilities, makes them quick and impulsive; but a lawyer is supposed to discriminate between what is specially benevolent and the obligations which we owe to the social compact: from him we expect to learn that an unlawful way of seeking a supposed good is fraught with a destructive principle, before which every thing may be laid waste. That compassion for a fugitive slave which leads one to abrogate the constitution of society is not benevolent, nor does it secure respect from any but radicals — a class of men, in all ages of the world, who have uniformly failed to secure the confidence of mankind.

CHAPTER XI.

NEW POSSIBLE ISSUES ON THE SUBJECT OF SLAVERY.

AND can there be no end to our division and strife with regard to this subject? Are we to spend the rest of this century debating it and contending over it? None can describe the vast harm which it has done to all our social relations. It has been the occasion of more unkind feelings and words, probably, than any other subject; it has alienated friends, divided great ecclesiastical communions, disturbed the peace of churches and parishes, led to the dismission of ministers, driven many into infidelity, embarrassed legislation, filled great sections of the country with jealousy of each other, consumed the strength and zeal which were needed to remedy evils among ourselves, and, at the present time, is threatening us with greater mischief than ever before.

The question which has hitherto absorbed our thoughts has been, "In what way shall slavery be disposed of consistently with the safety and interests of this nation?" This question seems as far as ever from a satisfactory answer.

Perhaps it may not be long before different questions will be forced upon our attention, which, while they will gratify and satisfy the interest of good men in the subject as moral and philanthropic questions, will unite us at the north, and also, by the national relation of the subject, with the south.

Let us then imagine for a few moments that the north and south, through some unforeseen harmonious influence, are actually losing all other thoughts upon this subject in their interest on this question, " What duties do the American people owe to the African race here and elsewhere?" It is a question which the providence of God, in the remarkable history and continuance of slavery in this country, may have intended, from the beginning, to force upon our attention.

We may be too impatient with regard to the continuance of American slavery. Mingled with the system there are mitigating elements which we do not sufficiently consider ; but above and beyond this there are hopeful and even cheerful views of it for those who will connect it with their belief in the sure progress of human redemption. The continuance to the present time of slavery, unprotected by old feudal institutions, but surrounded by the popular influences of such a land and such an age as this, its evident strength, its step advancing against such powerful opposition, must awaken thoughtfulness in the minds of all who are disposed to reflection. Is this system to be utterly abolished? or can it be that in some form it is connected, in the mysterious purposes of God, with his great plan of good will toward men, and especially toward the African race ? The contemplation of this question in a candid spirit will soothe our feelings and modify our views and measures with regard to this great national concern.

Could this question, in some practical form, get possession of the public mind, it is evident that antagonism between the north and south, on the subject of slavery, would soon be destroyed. "The expulsive power of a new affection," as a theologian has expressed it, is constantly illustrated in change of personal habits and character, in love, in business, and religion; attachments, seemingly invincible, to certain views, are at once and wholly destroyed by the entrance of a new master passion.

Never can the instincts of people unused to slavery be overcome by argument; never can the most law-abiding, patriotic submission at the north to the recovery of slaves cease to be accompanied, in the minds of many, with repugnance and distress, so long as they retain their present associations with slavery. On the other hand, a southerner, looking at the slaves from childhood, regarding the Constitution of the United States as the rule by which we are to be governed, can not appreciate our difficulties. Discussion may proceed without end and in vain. No limit seems possible to disagreement on the subject of slavery; claims founded upon it and resisted, irritating acts, and unkind, hostile words threaten to make the days of the years of the life of this nation, like those of Jacob, however protracted, seem few and evil. Some great question is capable of so absorbing our minds as to have all the effect of agreement on the subject, by leading us to act efficiently, and on a large scale, for the welfare of the African race here and on the continent of Africa.

The object is not to propose any way in which this may be effected, but merely to suggest the possibility of such relief. God can arrest the career of our present thoughts and purposes on this subject by some surprising event of his providence toward us or toward that people. His Spirit changes the views and feelings of individuals, makes entire revolutions in the opinions of whole communities, brings stillness and fear upon the hearts of men at the approach of divine judgments, fills multitudes with solemn religious impressions by means of some providential event. It is in his power to bring over the entire mind of this nation, agitated by the subject of slavery, a calm like that of twilight; he can make us drop our contentions and forget our differences by some influence of his, as at the curfew knell the Britons covered their fires. With men this is impossible ; legislation, ecclesiastical censures, compromises, discussions, political parties, can not do it; but it can be done by Him in whose works, at the beginning, darkness preceded the light, and by whose appointment, in private experience and in great national histories, it is the same now as when "the evening and the morning were the first day."

It would not be a more surprising event than the development of the California enterprise within a few years past, if some development in Africa should draw attention to it in connection with the employment of portions of our colored people there. The possibility of this, and of many other ways of relief which will occur to a reflecting mind, should help our faith and patience. Instead of contending with one another, and endangering our future means of doing good to the colored race through impatience at present and temporary evils, necessary, in the providence of God, as it may prove, to prepare us all for his further benevolent purposes, let us endeavor to heal the breaches between us, and interchange kind words and deeds.

Africa is still, to a great extent, a land of bondage. Three millions and a quarter of her children are slaves in Brazil, nine hundred thousand in the Spanish colonies, eighty-five thousand in the colonies of Holland, a hundred and forty thousand in European establishments in Africa, and over three millions in the United States.

Here, then, is a member of the human family whom God in his sovereignty has for five centuries suffered to bow its neck to other races. The susceptibility of these people to servitude should touch the hearts of their fellow-men, and stir them up to defend and protect them. The reverse of this has been the history of their treatment; but there is a day of redemption at hand; they will see good according to the days in which they have seen evil.

Amid all the tumultuous excitement on the subject of American slavery and the din of approaching conflict, I cannot help looking at the south as the appointed protectors of this feeble member of the human family. Brought to them indeed in transgression, and subjected to every injury, the importation of them protracted by northern votes eight years against the wishes of the south, the great law of human progress is nevertheless reaching them. Instead of regarding the south as holding their fellow-men in cruel bondage, let us consider whether we may not think of them as the guardians, educators, and saviors of the African race in this country.

Only they who have been brought up with them from childhood are qualified, as a general thing, to succeed well in the care and management of them. The common remark, that slaveholders from the free States are the worst masters, has honorable exceptions, owing to moral qualities in certain men which sustain them amidst great trials of patience; to which trials, ordinarily, one must have been used from infancy, not to be intolerant and severe toward the slaves. A man from New

England, accustomed to have his orders obeyed promptly and with the faithfulness which self-interest dictates, finds it hard to bear the slack manner of that " eye service " against which an Apostle admonishes " servants." If we are to do further good to the African race in this country, we must be obliged to our southern brethren and sisters to do it for us.

We frequently meet with the proposition to bring over Asiatic free laborers to supplant the Africans. If the object of this be to drive out slavery and the colored race with it, we shall gain nothing in the matter of races by taking the Asiatics in the place of the Africans, nor will the condition of the Asiatics here long be any more agreeable to them and to us than slavery now is.

The revival of the trade in African negroes is mentioned now and then at the south; but it will be in time to discuss that scheme when it is seriously entertained by any Christian nation.

Among the strange and extremely improbable things which are sometimes proposed, the voluntary immigration of Africans to our southern regions, if any one could bring it about and make it acceptable to the south, would no doubt be for the good of that race.

The immigration of Africans to the south would be better than that of coolies, or any other new race, while their labor might be equally cheap, being essentially free labor under strong regulations, and obviating the present enormous and increasing expense of buying the person of the colored man. It is by no means certain that some great change in the system of black labor, on account of the great prices demanded for slaves, will not be indispensable if the cotton interest in this country is to continue.

It is only because it is hardly safe to deny that any thing is possible, that we say it may turn out, after all, as some suppose, that God has ordained us to receive the African race still more extensively for their benefit and ours, as we already are as an asylum to the oppressed and poor of other lands. His plan seems to be, that suffering nations shall resort hither. As we give the wheat-growing districts to the Europeans, perhaps the tropical regions on this continent are to be the temporary abode of the African, from which he will go forth, as Moses did, to look upon his brethren and deliver them. How they are to come, and whether they will be received, is not considered.

We have reason to pause and wonder at the ill success, hitherto, of efforts to rid ourselves of the blacks; and moreover the providence of God, the God of nature and the God of nations, with respect to that great staple of commerce, our cotton, is worthy of consideration. It is not unfrequently the case that the word *cotton* is made a byword; it is spoken with a sneer; it is cotton, we are told, that keeps three millions in bondage, and it is denounced as the foe of human liberty. Now, the great God that formed all things has seen fit to connect that single product with the comfort and happiness of a large portion of the earth, and by its connection with mercantile exchanges, being eighty-six per cent of all that is raised on the whole earth, it exerts a preeminent influence upon the world's commerce. The rainy season in the East Indies occurs at a part of the year which makes it impossible for that district of the earth to compete with us in the supply of this article; we are appointed to this work; the south was about to free herself of her slaves; northern interference, seeking to hasten the day, prevented it, perhaps forever; and now we will not dispute with those who say that the south, and other portions of our land and continent, are, perhaps, to be the nursery of millions more of Africans, for their present and eternal good, and for the increasing supply of the world with a great necessary of life. Perhaps, in future, the failure of southern efforts at emancipation may be the occasion of unparalleled good to that race, by bringing us to unite in the only compromise that will save us from ruin and them from protracted misery. That which we do not know can not bring us much comfort; yet we admit that, could we bring the slaves, every where, through our example and efforts, under the social and religious influences which many of the slaves at the south enjoy, it would be, in fact, breaking every yoke. At all events, let us look above sectional and political considerations. There is a stone cut out of the mountains without hands which is destined to fill the earth. Oppression will flee before it; and whatever relation the colored man may sustain to the white man, it must be only such as will be for the benefit of both. We must not be prejudiced by our associations with the word *slavery*, but consider what the nature and influences of the relation designated by it are; and if necessary hereafter, whether our brethren, the colored men, may not be related to us even more extensively than now, as dependent objects of a benevolence which this nation will be so fully prepared to render, in view of the wrongs and woes of which we have been the occasion.

Then, the north and the south having a common aim with regard to the African race, every thing in the nature of oppressive laws made necessary by the self-defence of one section of the country against the other, and all usages not approved by an enlightened and benevolent mind, will be done away.

Then that cause of endless irritation and war, as things now are, escape from the south, will be harmoniously adjusted; and it is impossible to see in what other way it ever can cease to divide and embroil us.

Then the long-vexed question about the right of man to hold property in man will forever cease among us by our universal agreement to stand in the relation to the African as a stronger and more highly favored brother.

Then our brethren and friends, those noble and brave spirits who emigrate from us to the new Territories, instead of rushing to shut the gates against slaveholding immigrants, will be relieved of all apprehension of conflict by a general agreement what portions of our unsettled lands will be most favorable for the African race in connection with white men.

Then this most perplexing subject, which irritates and divides us against each other at the north, and arrays the north and west against the south, will be taken out of the way. God hasten it in his time.

We may yet thank and bless the south for being willing to continue her relation to the colored race; it may yet seem to us one of the greatest illustrations of divine wisdom in the affairs of men that she was prevented from throwing off the blacks.

Some of these reflections may serve to nourish hope, keep us from desperation or despondency, make us forbearing, and teach us to connect every thing in the affairs of the world with the beneficent plan of God and the sure law of human progress. No one can tell the result of this agitation on the subject of slavery;

but no one can consider its remarkable history and not feel that there may be some great design in it which will satisfy those who prefer the will of God to their own philosophy.

If any of the foregoing new schemes which are now afloat for the Africans may be pronounced visionary, as they seem to be, it is a relief, at least, to have a slight variety in our fanaticism on this subject, which has been more fruitful of fanaticism than any other subject in our history.

One thought only shall be added here. Past events teach us that this whole subject is a great deep; and we have had sufficient admonition to be very humble and patient as to future disclosures in connection with it. He who insists upon any definite scheme with regard to the subject seems as sure to draw upon himself a just suspicion of unsoundness of mind as he who professes to have a key to Daniel or the Apocalypse.

CHAPTER XII.

DISSUASIVE FROM INTERFERENCE WITH THE SOUTH.

THE north must take the first step in pacifying the country on this subject; and to some it will seem to be a backward step.

We must begin to be "friends of the master," if we would be truly "friends of the slave." Our only way of benefiting the slave is through his master.

Let us then think of that great body of Christian men at the south, who are perfectly competent to manage this subject, and meet their accountability to God without our help.

The Presbyterian, the Methodist, the Baptist, the Episcopal ministry there are a goodly fellowship of men, who, if drawn up over against us northern ministers, would strike a feeling of diffidence in us, to say the least, with regard to any bold, hasty imputation of injustice, cruelty, or enormous wrong; men who know more than we can tell them about the evils of slavery; who are incapable of being seduced or overawed by wickedness; and who are fully competent to struggle with the evils of the system, and to reform them, without one word of exhortation or advice from us; and whose daily prayer, with regard to us, is, that if there be any consolation in Christ, if any bowels of mercies, we would let them alone. Remember what they said and did before we drove them to personal self-defence. Mingle with them as friends, and not as antagonists; hear them preach and pray; talk with them as you loiter in the woods, or ride, or sail; and let them tell you, as they will be sure to do, all their burden on this subject, and compare it with what you see in the streets, and in families, and in all the unconstrained intercourse of society; and you will be sure to feel that the greatest kindness which we at the north can bestow upon the slaves, is to be no longer the seeming enemies, the censors, the civil and ecclesiastical judges of the masters.

We must, therefore, change our manner and tone with regard to the south, and study ways to signify such a change. One expression of kind feeling, one fraternal act on the part of the north toward the south, in exchange for the almost unremitted expressions of displeasure with which she is addressed, would do much to restore a good understanding, not by its influence at the south, but by putting ourselves into a more suitable attitude. Any thing like inviting the south to a compromise on this subject, or obtaining from her a promise that certain things shall be done on certain conditions, is absurd. We must of our own selves correct the spirit and manner in which we have conducted toward her.

Little things may involve great principles, and are connected with important effects; and therefore the following obvious illustration of what has now been said will not be considered trivial.

There is one form of unkindness and hardship inflicted on southerners, which, for the good effect the change would have upon ourselves, we shall do well to remove.

We will suppose that a husband at the north is advised to take his wife to the south for several months, to save, or at least, prolong life. She has a young and only child. There is a domestic in the family, between whom and the child there has been and is an attachment almost romantic, and in whom the parents place unlimited trust, who, besides her valuable services to the patient, will make the child happy, and so relieve the mother wholly of care. The privilege of taking such a domestic to a distant part of the country, under such circumstances, is beyond price.

Now, there are husbands and wives at the south in corresponding circumstances. To spend the hot season on our seaboard, or at the water-cures, seems necessary to save life. They have a colored nurse, who is to them all that the domestic just mentioned is in her place; and no one could be more. The nurse knows no happiness compared with ministering to this family; but she is in law a slave. A slave can not set foot in Massachusetts, for example, without being, by that act, free, and may go or come at pleasure. Were this family sure that no inducements would be offered to draw this nurse away from them clandestinely, they would take the risk of her deserting them. But to have a vigilance committee about their premises at the north, tampering with the woman; to miss their nurse suddenly when their need may be sorest; to follow the habeas corpus and the crowd to court; and to be gazetted, and to see the happiness for life of an estimable servant put in jeopardy through some powerful temptation, or sudden indiscretion, induces them to forego the privilege of taking her with them, and either to endure the trouble and risk of obtaining a suitable nurse at the north, or to stay at home.

It is easy to see that there is a large amount of inconvenience and suffering occasioned by such liabilities, which is not of course published, but to which northerners would submit with very poor grace. We desire to guard against the possibility of slavery being reëstablished in Massachusetts, as might be the case if slaves were brought into the State to remain indefinitely, at the pleasure of the master or mistress. This self-defence we can not yield. But it seems hard if some good understanding can not be had, to the effect that travelers from the south, visitors, are to be protected in the enjoyment of services rendered by members of their families, who, if left to themselves, would not exchange their condition, with its name slavery, for any thing under the name of freedom. Now, they must either stay at home or leave their favorite servants behind them — the skillful driver, the almost physician, who has dressed the chronic sore for months; the maid, who is a rival with the mother in the child's love; this must be foregone, because of our practice of waylaying with the habeas corpus every colored servant from the south.

Let our people be appealed to against this injustice and unkindness. Legislation can not well remedy the evil, especially if its only remedy be the poor donation of leave to stay a few weeks, and no more, with a slave at the north, as some of the free States have enacted. This concession makes visitors from the south feel that they are under obligations to us for that which ought not to be placed on the ground of permission.

Would that, for our own sakes, we could enjoy the pleasure more frequently of becoming acquainted with the citizens of the south in their domestic relations. We are becoming mutually repulsive, through northern jealousy and fear. Are we afraid that the sight of the happy relation subsisting between masters and their slaves will make our people in love with the institution? Would that all could see instances of such relationships under this system. It would do much toward abolishing things objectionable in slavery, by making us discriminating and just in our censure, if there should be need of any. It would do much toward satisfying us that the south is competent to manage this subject without our help.

As a dissuasive from interference with the south with regard to slavery, it is deeply interesting to consider the impulses of their intelligent and good men in measures of relief and kindness toward the colored people.

Notwithstanding the powerful pressure from jealousy of northern interference with which these impulses are obliged to contend, philanthropy is working out benevolent plans for the slaves.

Men at the south, in places of influence, whose opinions have a controlling effect, are meditating the following changes, among others, in the slave code.

One is, to raise the term of years within which no child shall be separated from its parents. The age proposed in the case to which I allude, and which would have been adopted by the legislature had it not been for some appeals with regard to northern interference, was thirteen. In that State, a child over five years of age may now be separated from its parents.

Another proposition generally entertained is, to forbid the sale of a slave for debt. This would prevent, of course, a vast proportion of painful separations. It would greatly change the nature of slavery.

Another proposition is, that slaves shall by law have

a right of release from a cruel master, as provided for by slave codes of some other nations.

In recent numbers of the New Orleans Crescent we find a series of articles in favor of giving the right of suffrage to the native free colored population.

But the most interesting and important proposition which is discussed in some quarters is that of legalizing the marriage of slaves. There is a strong sentiment in favor of this measure.

Surely there is progress in a right direction at the south; and may we at the north but exercise wisdom and discretion, we shall soon see great changes in favor of the colored race. These changes have begun where slavery has felt the influence of the best state of society; but they will in time reach the relation of master and slave in all the land.

Let us grant for a moment all that the strongest advocates of the right and duty of intervention by the north with southern slavery have ever claimed. It shall be allowed that we are accountable to God for every oppression which exists in our slave States, and that our first duty, to which no claims at home, even, are superior, is, to see that this system of slavery is virtually abolished. What is the best way to accomplish the object?

We have tried one method for more than a quarter of a century. So long we have been practising upon our patient, and to-day the disease is extending more rapidly than ever. Some practitioners would, in such a case, have misgivings about the mode of treatment; and we may well indulge a similar distrust.

If the object be to subdue the south as a political enemy, and abridge her influence in the general government, the only way is to plot and counterplot against her by means of political organizations and party warfare, and leave every thing to the fortunes of the war.

But is it the sincere and kind desire of any to see the supposed wrongs and woes of the colored race redressed, and our system of slavery purged of every objectionable influence, and thus, if in no other way, to prevent it from further afflicting the white and black races? Is this the form of our antislavery? Does this express the substance of our abolitionism?

We are sitting down like an army before an impregnable wall, battering the gates and throwing bombs promiscuously into the place. A strong party within are in principle essentially with us, and, if suffered to exert their influence unmolested from without, would effect all that we desire. As it is, they are opposed to have their houses and lives destroyed by our indiscriminate shot, nor are they willing that we should march in and give laws. Therefore they combine with their civil opponents to resist their military assailants. Never will they cease to resist and oppose us, not for our principles, but for our mode of enforcing them. If conquest be not our aim, or the gratification of malignant passions, but simply to have justice executed, our surest way to effect this is, to withdraw our forces, and leave the cause in the hands of those who but for us would long since have made their influence effectual. This will not prevent us from using all proper measures of simple self-defence. To do more than this, under existing circumstances, is to perpetuate the evil which we would see removed.

There are many things in slavery which, as human beings, fellow-creatures with the slaves, we intensely desire to see abolished. Let no man say here, " Why

take an interest in my servants?" But if he says
this, we will remind him of a well-known scene in a
Roman theatre, where these words of a former slave, " I
am a man, and nothing that pertains to man do I consider as not pertaining to me," brought down thunders
of applause. We reciprocate, for all his fellow-servants
and fellow-men every where, the noble sentiment of this
slave; nor would pagan Rome reprove us. Every week,
events within the bounds of slavery make us cry out to
know what can be done to prevent them. Tell us, friends
and brethren at the south, what shall we at the north do,
or cease to do, to help you prevent these enormities?
The last that came to the knowledge of some of us was
a well-authenticated case, in which forty persons, descendants of a freed slave, some of whom had been free
for thirty years, were to be reduced again to slavery, on
the claim of one man. Can you do nothing to prevent
such things? Can we help you, either by act or by
silence? Tell us if we have any duty whatever in the
case. If it were the Greeks, or the Poles, or the starv-
ing Irish, or the Madiai, who were suffering these things,
you and we would inquire at the capital whether, as a
nation, we had no call to interfere.

We do not wish to be contending against brethren and
friends in a good cause. We can not desire to perpetuate,
by our well-meant endeavors, the evils which you and
we seek to remove. Who of you, then, will speak out,
and, recognizing the evils to which we allude, show us
our duty? Be sure that your directions will be grate-
fully received and honorably regarded.

It is appalling to think of a presidential campaign in
which the subject of slavery, with its potent sway over
human passions, shall be the all-absorbing question. We

are going into battle with conscience exalted to absolute monarchy and dictatorship; conscience, under whose banner, in the name of God, wars, persecutions, tortures, and massacres have made the earth reel, and the blood of saints has reached to the horses' bridles. The destiny of unborn millions, as slaves or free, will excite one party beyond all former experience, and under the combined heat of conscience, humanity, fancy, sectional feelings, fanaticism, and recollections of recent defeat in the Nebraska measure, even adamantine bonds will melt. On the other hand, domestic institutions, homes, the whole mysterious, complicated system of life, in one entire and united section of the country, will arm fifteen States of the Union with a desperation such as they only feel who are in the agony of a last hope.   Let us not see that contest.   " The shields of the earth belong unto the Lord."

There is such a mixture of political and moral questions in this subject of slavery, that no one can tell by what motives men are influenced in their opposition.   Some, whose thoughts and purposes are wholly political, nevertheless make use of our sensibility to the moral relations of the subject, and complicate the bare question of the moral character of slavery with appointments to foreign political offices, and the customs, and post-offices.   Thus they justly incur the opposition of the south by their invectives against slavery, when their chief objection to it is the influence which it exerts in the government. Could the subject become a simple moral question, and be discussed apart from politics, the jealousy and opposition of the south would have far less excitement.   The best thing which we at the north can do to pacify the country, to help the colored race, to prevent further

Nebraska measures, and promote our common interests as a nation, is to reconsider our feelings and conduct in times past toward the south. A penitential state of mind becomes us. In that statesman's manual, the Bible, there is a passage of history most pertinent in its application to us at the north. The tribe of Benjamin had been guilty of an " enormous wrong " in the case of the Levite and his concubine. The other tribes assembled before God, prepared for war. Their question was, " Which of us shall go up first to the battle against Benjamin ? " Not, Shall we go up ? nor, In what way shall we best bring the offender to repentance?

The answer was in anger. Thrice Israel was smitten, and at last the offending tribe was defeated, with a slaughter on both sides, in the three battles, of sixty-five thousand men. Then the nation wept over the almost ruined tribe, and resorted twice to the stealing of women from neighboring people to repair it.

So much for unwarrantable methods of redressing " enormous wrongs " in the bosom of a nation.

Let it be repeated, we must not seek to obtain from the south any expression in the way of confession, or concession, or promise. We are not properly a ruler or a judge over them, though we have assumed both offices. Let us adopt the principle that the south is competent to manage the subject of slavery, and straightway cease from all offensive action. Proper defences for free colored citizens must be secured, and, if sought for, disconnected with the agitation of the subject of slavery, as a political or sectional interest, can unquestionably be obtained. We must put a stop to the unlawful seizure of colored servants passing with their masters through a free State. We must in some way prevent the annoyance to which southern travelers are exposed of having their colored servants enticed away, or brought before the courts to be emancipated. Perhaps these things, in connection with our whole manner of treating the south, have created a state of mind in which it was easy to violate compromises.

Two things they do not ask nor expect of us, viz., to express any approbation of slavery, nor to sympathize with them. A northerner at the south soon perceives that, if he feels and shows in a proper manner a natural repugnance to slavery, they respect him for it, while they greatly suspect and distrust those from the north who seem in favor of the system. Moreover, any condolence with them at the evils of slavery, or show of interposition for their benefit, is wholly out of place.

A slaveholder of liberal education and great influence at the south, and withal an extreme defender of the system of slavery, made a declaration, which, for many reasons, impressed me, perhaps, more than any thing which fell from the lips of a southerner. He said, "If the north had directed its strength against the evils of slavery instead of assailing it as a sin *per se*, it could not have survived to the present day." This is confirmed by many witnesses, and may teach us wisdom in time to come.

But our invectives against the south, our exaggerated representations of slavery, our indiscriminate imputations of connivance with its abuses, our political opposition, our resistance of southern rights under the Constitution, and our efforts to decoy the servants, at home and abroad, excite opposition which renders all our desire for the benefit of the colored race in this country entirely hopeless. We may drive the south and her slaves from the Union, but we thereby gain nothing for the slaves.

CHAPTER XIII.

INFLUENCE OF UNCLE TOM'S CABIN AT HOME AND ABROAD.

ONE thing which interested me at the south was the spirit in which Uncle Tom's Cabin was frequently mentioned. Some of the warmest advocates of slavery said that they could parallel most of the abuses in slavery mentioned in the book out of their own knowledge; and on speaking of some bad master, and wishing to express his tyrannical character and barbarous conduct, they would say, He is a real Legree; or, He is worse than Legree. The book was mentioned with candor, and with little appearance of wounded sensibility. Yet many criticisms were made upon it, both of a sectional and general nature.

There was one criticism on the plan of the book which may be heard from every southerner, even from those among them who are antislavery men. The scene with which the book opens, they say, is unnatural. A gentleman embarrassed and constrained to sell a slave, and especially a child, would not act the part of Mr Shelby, in that conversation and drinking scene which are described in the first chapter. If, by the strangest combination of events, he should be led to do it, he would fling himself, with such a slave and child, into the hands of a trader, in the same state of mind with which he would surrender his wife's wardrobe, or her jewelry, inherited from her mother; but to sit and laugh, and hold up the glass, and uncork a new bottle of wine, and peel an orange, and haggle with a fiend like Haley, they say, is not according to human nature among slaveholders, in any man who had not himself become a fiend. But above all, to represent a southern gentleman, a man having "the appearance of a gentleman," "the arrangements of the house and the general air of the housekeeping indicating easy and even opulent circumstances," as suffering Haley to bid for such a woman as Eliza, with a view to her peculiar fitness for the New Orleans market, "slapping Mr. Shelby on the shoulder," and coaxing him to let him have her for this purpose, it may well be conceived by honorable and virtuous gentlemen, is felt to be an affront by every decent man at the south — a coarse, broad, disgusting caricature, which, as a libel on a community, they say, hardly has a parallel.

The tone of fairness with which the book is mentioned at the south makes one feel that they have reasons in their consciousness for protesting as they do against this part of the book, or rather this part of its plan. The manner in which the criticism is made gives one a favorable and deep impression of the relation between a master and a good slave ; it is not a mercenary relation. This impression is confirmed every day in the mind of a visitor, until, on reperusing the opening scene in Uncle Tom, he finds that the representation of a southerner with "the appearance of a gentleman, in easy and even opulent circumstances," in connection with the abominable talk and purposes of that scene, is an imposition and a cruel injustice.

While many things in the book are paralleled by characters and events at the south, and while the Key more than proves it, still, like all other novels, it deceives. At the north I partook fully in the general effect of the book upon our feelings, as the author knows full well; but at the south, even after seeing or hearing things like many which are related in the story, I found that still the whole impression of the book on my mind was that of a falsehood. Perhaps this was in part my fault as a reader; it is in part the fault of novel writing, its intrinsic evil.

The first thing in which I found myself misled by the impressions to which I had yielded in the book, was with respect to the children of the slaves. I had fixed the image of Topsy in my mind as the exponent of colored children, and of Eva as their contrast. I supposed that generally a black child was, as Topsy said of herself, "nothing but a nigger" in its own esteem and that of the whites. I expected to find in those black children imps, Shakspeare's Calibans and Flibbertigibbets, a provoking, disgusting brood. I was angry with myself to find how I had suffered poor Topsy to form my notions of childhood and youth among the slaves; but I may be alone in the impression which she had the misfortune to give me of her race. I saw specimens of some, who, with a little change, in the hands of a fictitious writer, would answer for Topsys — girls as disagreeable and impracticable as their prototype; but they are the exceptions; there is such a class; Topsy is a fact; and this is all which the volume intended to say, and by no means to libel the whole rising generation among the slaves, by setting forth Topsy to represent them to the world. But notwithstanding the writer's good intentions, she did

not, she could not limit the influence of her book upon
the fancies and feelings of her readers. I found myself
frequently stopping to talk with the black children, for
the pleasure of hearing them talk, and secretly feeling
also, that I owed them some atonement for the injustice
which I had done to them in my thoughts.

The next thing in which I found myself repenting of
the impressions which, with no such design on the part
of the writer, the book had given me, was with regard
to the influence of slavery on female character. I did
not suppose that Mrs. St. Clair was a true picture of
southern women, for I knew better; at the same time,
when I saw the women of the south in their families, on
their plantations, in their Sabbath schools, and heard
them speak of their servants, and found them making
the garments worn by field hands, superintending the
distribution of food, nursing the sick, and enduring toils
for them to which northern ladies are generally strangers, I felt that that miserable woman was out of place in
any prominent connection with descriptions of southern
character. Many, of course, were the instances in which
a character illustrating the entirely opposite effects of
slaveholding upon the women of the south occurred to
me, and so had they done to the narrator of Mrs. St.
Clair's biography; all that I would say is, I wondered
that such a woman should have been permitted to be
the prominent figure among her sex in the antislavery
romance. The writer's object was by no means to describe southern women; no one more than she would
deplore unjust impressions with regard to them derived
from her writings; yet one who has received the natural
impression of the book will find at the south that he dis--
likes Mrs. St. Clair, for new reasons, more than ever.

And then, as a whole, I found that the book gives a northerner false conceptions of the actual state of things at the south, not excepting abuses in slavery; for with respect even to them, after reading the book, apparitions will be ever present to one's thoughts, which will not be laid except by going south. There he sees that many things referred to can and may take place; but if he has taken the book into his mind almost as a traveler in the East takes the book of Joshua, if he expects frequently or necessarily to pattern after the book in his observations, he will be displeased with himself more than with the writer at his mistake.

By using any simile to illustrate what has now been said, there is danger of doing to the reader what the book in question does to us. But it occurred to me that Uncle Tom's Cabin was in some sense like a solar microscope applied to vinegar. Fearful are the sights thus revealed in that liquid. Lizards, ichthyosaurians, and megalatheria in general, are there without number; and the impression is, that the element in which they live is appropriate to their dispositions, for they are evidently carrying on an internecine war. Are not those things there? will you dispute the evidence of sight? is it not the essential nature of vinegar to generate such things? and will you ever taste a drop of vinegar hereafter? This simile is capable of great perversion and abuse; and so is the author's design in the Cabin.

The truth is, the writer of Uncle Tom's Cabin is not only the foe, but the Defoe, of slavery, and Uncle Tom is the Robinson Crusoe of involuntary servitude. Now, if people, as far as possible from the seaboard, should ask me for a book giving a true picture of a sailor's experience, it would be as fair to give them Robinson

Crusoe as to put Uncle Tom's Cabin into the hands of a
foreigner who wished to learn what American slavery actually is.   Robinson Crusoe is all probable, has all been
verified ; but the journals of our merchantmen do not
ordinarily correspond with the experiences of that book,
and still every crew, in every voyage, is liable to verify
it for substance, in every part of the earth.

Having written the foregoing at the south, I was
much interested a week or two afterwards, on receiving
the Boston Daily Advertiser, in meeting with the following coincidence of opinion and expression in an
article by one of the respected editors of that paper,
being a notice of an article in the North American
Review for April, on Robinson Crusoe : —

" Robinson Crusoe has a peculiar interest to American
students, because properly an American novel, written by
a Puritan, with its locality, scenery, and moral all strictly
American.   It is worth remark that the play Shakspeare
is said to have valued most was the Tempest, whose
scenery is all American also.   The greatest English romance and the greatest English drama are ours, the first
fruits of the new world to English literature.
  " We are tempted to add, as a suggestion to his next re-
viewer, that Robinson Crusoe, and the only other English
romance which has ever attained an equal popular circulation, — both novels of American life, — illustrate together
the vanity of ' the argument from invented example,' or
rather the ease with which fiction may be turned to support either side of a moral question.
  " Uncle Tom's Cabin — the only romance which has
gained a popular circulation equal to Robinson Crusoe —
is the history of a slave, written to expose, and wonder-
fully successful in exposing, the horrors of the slave
system.   Robinson Crusoe, on the other hand, whom every
reader loves, was a slave trader, shipwrecked on a voyage to the Guinea coast for slaves, which he never re-
gretted for its wickedness ; and one of the features of his
life for which certainly he is least blamed, is his holding

Friday, whom he has preserved (*servus quia servatus erat*) as his slave. The Christian slave Uncle Tom and the Christian slaveholder Robinson Crusoe are the two most popular heroes of English romance. So little is really proved by the argument from invented example."

Let us imagine an intelligent community in Southern India, where custom, we will suppose, had for generations forbidden widowers with children to marry. The proposition being made to set aside this custom, some, who are still in favor of the prohibition, cause to be translated and circulated a book written in America called the Stepmother. It is a novel. The author having been deeply affected by the acknowledged misery resulting in very many cases, from the injustice and cruelty of stepmothers, constructs a most thrilling tale, which makes more weeping than any book of its time. Objections having been made to the representations in the book, the author gives a Key in which she prints authentic letters detailing scenes of exquisite domestic misery in consequence of second marriages. Her novel is most fully sustained by these cases ; and indeed the one half has not been told.

Perhaps the nucleus of the story was furnished by a transaction which we all know to be true, and which at the time made a sensation that needed no aid from fancy. An adopted boy told his father of some improprieties which he had accidentally witnessed in his stepdame in connection with a gentleman. The wife denied it, and required that the boy be whipped for falsehood. The father was deacon of a church. He whipped the little fellow till a pool of blood stood at his feet, the child protesting his innocence and truthfulness ; and with his dying accents, (for he died,) after saying, "I feel cold," as the chill of death came over him, he said, "Dear father, I love you." The two parents were at the last accounts in jail awaiting their trial. I give the narrative from memory; a fictitious case would serve my purpose, but this appeared in an authentic manner not long since in the papers. The writer of the fiction which we are supposing would need to alter this case so far as to call this adopted child an own child of this father, and the woman a stepmother. But, for the vast good which was meant to be accomplished, how few fictitious writers would consider it wrong to make even so essential an alteration!

No fictitious narrative of slavery or piracy could make a deeper impression than a book on this subject written by a female hand which knew well how to touch the chords of the human heart, especially if there were interspersed skillful representations of the unnaturalness of second love, of the impossibility that maternal affection should be imitated, and that where a stepmother has children of her own, there is the strongest temptation to partiality, with other theoretically truthful things which a woman of genius would know so well how to set forth. The book, then, is published in India.

Should visitors in India from America be reproached with this picture of domestic life in second marriages, and should they complain that it is unjust, every mouth could be stopped by the question, "Is there a word in the book which is not true? Do you deny the facts?"

It would all be true; but the common law adage would apply, in a sense different, it is true, from its intended meaning, "The greater the truth, the greater the libel."

Husbands and fathers who have found for their motherless children second mothers whose disinterested, im-

partial, generous love for their stepchildren approaches
nearer than any thing else on earth to the ministry of
angels, must feel that such a book, with all its candid
and fair protestations in favor of the many exceptions
to the general rule of the unnaturalness of second marriages and second mothers, would make a false impression in a country where the whole truth could not be
known, the necessity of second marriages be appreciated,
and the incidental evils of the relation in question, and
its abuses, be distinguished from its normal operation
under moral and Christian principle.

How natural and kind it would be for the women of
India, led by that accomplished woman, the lady Rajah
Seringapatam, to join in an address to the stepmothers
of the United States, deploring the existence of such
enormous wrongs, and remonstrating with their Christian
sisters! If the burning of widows on the same funeral
piles with the bodies of their husbands were at the date
of the address still practised, the sympathy of those East
Indian women with our domestic histories would be better appreciated, especially if the suttees should be passed
over with but a slight allusion.

Now, it is not necessary to my argument that this case
should be shown to be parallel with slaveholding and
with a book written to show the evils of slavery. The
only point of the illustration (and let nothing else be
confounded with it) is this — that the truth, fairly, dis-
criminatingly, kindly spoken, and confirmed by more
than sufficient cases, the truth itself may operate most
cruelly if presented in the form of fictitious narrative.
This is an illustration, to those who wish to use it, of the
pernicious influence of novels. We can not describe a
character or class of men in any place without imprint-

ing almost the whole surface of a reader's mind with the image of the persons described, so as to fill his vision whenever he hears of or sees that place. Not to seem like laying blame on the writer of the book in question as a sinner above all others, but rather to comfort her in view of the harm she has done, by a somewhat flattering illustration, it may be observed that, passing through Coventry, England, I was sure that I saw survivors of Falstaff's ragged regiment; and whoever has read Shakspeare will find them there to-day. One man, in particular, stood as a specimen of them in the public square, at six o'clock in the morning, in the position of erect and somewhat opened dividers, his hands in his pockets, his coat torn under the right shoulder behind. I made no question that he was a survivor of his regiment. " I'll not march through Coventry with them," said Falstaff. But I could not help thinking that he did, and that some of them had never left the place. That ancient regiment, and Shakspeare, and " Peeping Tom," are no more to blame for our having few other thoughts at first in Coventry except those which are ludicrous, than are the Haleys and their inventor, and " Uncle Tom," for making us project the images of those characters all about us at first in the slaveholding States.

While we confine the influence of this imagination to our private thoughts, the practical evil, of course, is limited, though it is an evil; for it is not the truth; it is not the case as it exists.

But when this wrong impression, innocently made, instead of being left like a fugitive water color, becomes like a water color which is rolled over with a chemical preparation to sink and fix it; when a romance is followed by a book of facts to prove the tale, and this originally

wrong impression becomes an exasperated conviction
leading us to take counsel and revolutionize a country,
to exscind whole communities, to fill the air over their
heads with imprecations to Heaven for vengeance upon
them — it behooves us to pause and see whether our
premises are true; whether other things equally true do
not so modify the case, as presented in the novel, that
the fiction becomes false and injurious. With all my
feelings in favor of the work referred to, and against
our system of slavery, on going to the south as a place of
refuge in sickness with no purpose to become in any
wise interested in the subject of slavery, but rather
studying how to defend myself against the impressions
which I supposed it would make upon me, I found myself, for three months, in a state of society, in different
places, which made me say, " If Uncle Tom's Cabin is
true, there are other things just as true which ought to
modify every judgment of slavery as dictated by that
book."

The reply to this is, " You saw the best specimens of
slaveholding." Truly, I did; and gave thanks for the
power of the gospel in its direct and indirect influences
upon the master and slave. I took courage in thinking
what that gospel would continue to do there, if " the
wrath of man " could only be taught that it " worketh
not the righteousness of God." But if the remark im-
plies that I did not see and feel the evils of slavery, some
of the preceding pages, I trust, are a sufficient answer.

Indignity to the human person, meek sufferings under
cruelty, woman in the power of a brutal nature, childhood's innocence and simplicity, maternal instincts, the
pathetic themes of redemption, with interchanges of
drollery and brogue, that stroke of art to keep the sol-

emn and pathetic from palling upon the mind, and the didactic from seeming prosy, — these, combined by the hand of genius into a novel to make southern slavery abhorred, create an impression against the south itself which many can not see and feel to be in a most important sense, and to a great extent, unjust, till they mingle with the masters and servants. Had I read a novel designed to eulogize and commend the system, written with the power of this book, my disappointment and revulsion in another direction would have been no less real, though producing a different effect upon my feelings.

This book has entered like an alcoholic distillation into the veins and blood of very many people in the free States. They did not, nor do they now, make any distinction between Red River and any other river, south, or south-west; nor did the author mean that they should, for the Key applies the whole power of the book against slavery in all the south, and brings facts from the Southern States generally to corroborate the fiction.

At the south its effect is more secret. There are injuries which pride forbids men to retaliate at a time or in a way which will show that they are capable of being offended by them. In the secret places of the heart, the smothered fire slowly generates heat, which makes combustion fierce when the flame kindles. This book has had much to do with preparing a state of feeling at the south by which Nebraska measures are more willingly sustained. Yet most southerners would scorn the thought of being offended or influenced from such a source.*

* It will illustrate this topic to speak of Rev. Dr. Perkins's sermon preached at Oroomiah, Persia, entitled "Our Country's Sin."

But what impression must the book have made on foreign nations, was a question which occurred to me, if its impression on an American be thus false ? What ideas must Frenchmen, and the Swiss, and Germans, and the converts from heathenism and paganism, have of our southern men universally, if, for example, Topsy gave me such impressions respecting the slave children as a race of chimney sweeps ?

This question had ceased to interest me, for I had concluded that my own impressibility was in some way wrong, and that no one else would fall into the same error.

On looking at "Sunny Memories of Foreign Lands,"

Private letters from abroad inform us that it was written under the influence of the Cabin. A word of personal explanation will be excused. Dr. Perkins quotes from a sermon of mine on Mr. Webster the words, " Let the land have a Sabbath on this subject, (slavery,) and let this Sabbath be the long, long days of our mourning," &c., and he devotes some space, and uses strong language, in lamenting and reproving the idea of keeping " a Sabbath silence " with regard to slavery. My previous sentence would seem to make this meaning of my language improbable: " And now, as we sail away from the sea-girt tomb of our pilot, let us all agree, north, south, east, and west, to throw into the waves, as a sacrifice, our unkind feelings and bitter words on the subject of American slavery. Let the land have a Sabbath with regard to this subject," — meaning, and no doubt I should have added these words, *as thus discussed;* the idea of silence on this or any other great moral question being foreign from my thoughts. The blame of this sermon must not be laid at the door of that far-off mission home, with its privations and sorrows, but at the door of the Cabin, which led a missionary of the cross to employ the sacramental occasion to pour out his excruciated feelings to his little company of exiled brethren in reproof of pastors and religious editors here at home, whose chief, if not their only regret at the sermon, is the pain which it must have cost him to write and preach it. We are not offended. We can not, indeed, call his smiting of us " excellent oil," yet, like such oil, it has not broken our heads.

I came to this passage in the author's account of what she saw and heard in Geneva, Switzerland, at Castle Chillon : —

"After we left the dungeons, we went up into the judgment hall, where prisoners were tried, and then into the torture chamber. Here are pulleys by which limbs were broken ; the beam, all scorched with the irons by which feet were burned ; the oven where the irons were heated ; and there was the stone where they were sometimes laid to be strangled after the torture. On that stone, our guide told us, two thousand Jews, men, women, and children, had been put to death. There was also, high up, a strong beam across, where criminals were hung, and a door, now walled up, by which they were thrown into the lake. I shivered. ' 'Twas cruel,' she [the guide] said ; ' 'twas almost as cruel as your slavery in America.' "
"Then she took us into a tower," &c. — Vol. ii. pp. 273, 274.

Here I found that my false impressions with regard to slavery, made by reading the Cabin were probably not peculiar, and that, without doubt, unjust impressions have been given by the book to millions of foreign people. The torments of Chillon Castle, organized, administered religiously, scientifically, and with that diabolical cruelty in which passion has given place to stolid indifference, these are, in the view of a Swiss reader of the Cabin, "almost as cruel as your slavery in America." No rebuke, no correction is given. And all this time that the book is making these impressions with regard to the slaves, those slaves, notwithstanding the inherent evils and liabilities of their state, surpass any three millions of laboring people, in any foreign land, in comforts, in freedom from care, in provision for the future, in religious privileges and enjoyment, and probably send tenfold more from their number to be in heaven kings and priests to God.

In view of the injury inflicted on the south by this novel in the opinions and feelings of humane people all over the earth, the meekness and kindness with which it has been privately spoken of by many southerners awaken sympathy and love toward them, which, though slow, may one day overtake the injustice, and make compensatory reaction.

Many things in the book are specifically true; it has afforded an inestimable amount of pleasure; the author has been placed by it in situations of rich enjoyment, for which every generous mind is glad: and now we wish that the same genius might be employed in doing justice to private characters at the south, to the benevolent effects, in the providence of God, and the possible prospective relations, of slavery — slavery as it really is — slavery as it may be.

But the genius that dictated the Cabin would fail here. There would be no bad passions to be stimulated; hatred of the south would not be stirred; the self-righteousness of foreign people would be disturbed by the dark shade into which the bright side of slavery would throw their laboring poor. No political party, no rival religious publication societies, would get any help from it; certain aspirants for the presidency would, by its influence, see their prospects as in the light of a waning moon. Some would even burn the book on their platform with the Constitution of the United States. Infidels and atheists, who every year in May drink together the Circean cup of radicalism, would trample her book under their feet, and turn again and rend her. How she would use her well-known facility in quoting Scripture then: " My soul is among lions; and I lie even among them that are set on fire, whose teeth are spears and arrows, and their tongue a sharp sword."

The book will have the effect to make slaveholders, in many instances, feel the vast responsibleness which rests upon them to render to their servants that which is just and equal, knowing that they also have a Master in heaven, and that the world looks on to see how they use a trust by which they can do more good or more harm directly to a human being than in any other relation except that of a parent.

Now that we are upon this subject, something may be said, perhaps to good effect,—as certainly it is dictated by kind feelings in which personal attachments also mingle, —with regard to the manner in which the south and our country are spoken of, through the influence of northern hostility to slavery, not only by Americans, but by foreigners. Southerners have need of patience in view of the manner in which they are commonly spoken of by many. There is a saucy way of talking about slaveholders, a slurring manner of alluding to them in the style of byword, which ought to be reproved. The book already quoted, Sunny Memories, &c.,* affords an illustration of this in the Journal of the author's brother, who may as well be quoted for a casual example as any man, and who knows how to answer for himself. He is describing his altercation with a mule which had suddenly refused to move; he stones him in three distinct pitched onsets, each graphically described, and we hope in an exaggerated manner; for, had some southern gentlemen been passing by, they would have said, 'Were you a passionate negro, we should reprove you; but being one of the prominent exposers to the world of southern inhumanity, it must of course be all right.' The mule, in

* Vol. ii. pp. 257, 258.

one of his caprices, does some obstinate thing, and his
driver then compares him to "a proslavery demagogue."
His mode of dealing with the mule was so much like the
way in which, doubtless, he has heard some men reason
with the south, that while employed in showering granite
upon the dumb beast, proslavery men were readily suggested to his thoughts. The trimmings of low discourse
with some whom he can call to mind are flings at slaveholders. How strange it would seem to hear certain
men speak of slaveholders with courtesy, and of their
alleged sins with Christian sorrow, or even with a Christian indignation.

As specimens of the unjust manner in which our
country is regarded and spoken of under the influence
of certain representations of slavery, the following instances are in place. In this last-named book we read
that, —

"Madam Belloc received, a day or two since, a letter
from a lady in the old town of Orleans, which gave name
to Joan of Arc, expressing the most earnest enthusiasm in
the antislavery cause. Her prayers, she says, will ascend
night and day for those brave souls in America who are
conflicting with this mighty injustice." — Vol. ii. p. 416.

The question arises, "Who are these brave souls?"
We know, probably, to whom this refers; but what claim
have they to be called brave? They have said a great
many brave things, but have they done any? They have
added the great State of Texas to slave territory, and
this is characteristic of their history; their efforts have
all redounded to prevent emancipation, and strengthen
and extend slavery. They are like an army with no
weapons but boomerangs, which, before reaching the
object, turn in the air, and come back in the faces of those

who hurl them. For ill-adapted, unsuccessful efforts, no party ever made such an impression upon bystanders. Deborah would have felt obliged to upbraid them as she did Reuben in her war; Elijah, seeing them leaping on their altar at their anniversary, crying and cutting themselves, would have bid them cry louder; while as to some of their number who kept not their first estate, the apostle Jude could most appropriately have characterized and denounced them. They fling the Bible across the platform; impiously boast on whom they would put their feet, if He should teach otherwise than their resolutions have it; then pause for a poor non-resistant but extra-clamorous fanatic to be lifted out of doors by his hands and heels, when they proceed to assail that church of which they have been forewarned from the beginning that they should " never prevail against it."

The rest of us in this land, in the view of estimable foreigners whose knowledge with regard to our slaves began and ended in the Cabin, are a cruel, prejudiced, besotted people, upholding a mighty injustice, while a few "brave souls," comprising most of the piety and humanity in the United States, are contending with us at fearful odds in the spirit of Christian heroes.

In another part of the book the author describes a class of Americans in Paris who plunge into the stream of fashion and pleasure, and "speak with heartless levity of the revolutions in France as of a pantomime got up for their diversion:" they are "young America, fresh from the theatres and gambling saloons, declaring, between the whiffs of his cigar, that the French are not capable of free institutions; that the government of Louis Napoleon is the best thing France could have, " and dividing the time between defences of American slavery and efforts to attach themselves to the skirts of French tyranny." Having described this class of men, the writer remarks, —

" Thus from the plague spot at her heart has America become the propagandist of despotism in Europe." — Vol. ii. p. 418.

These few young gentlemen of the town, then, are America's representatives, for whose judgments and flashy sayings all the north, and west, and south are responsible, and by whom we are " propagating despotism," because, before they sailed for Paris, the country had not been able to agree as to the proper light in which to regard and treat the subject of slavery. For very many private reasons, it is painful to make these reflections; but it is time to see if we can not arrest the hurtful way in which some speak of their country in connection with slavery, or, at least, to let the more sensible among them see how their mode of speaking strikes some among their friends, of whose candor and kindness they have had sufficient proof. Here is an illustration : —

" In the course of the afternoon a telegraph came from the mayor of Liverpool, to inquire if our party would accept a public breakfast at the town hall, before sailing, as a *demonstration of sympathy with the cause of freedom.*" — Vol. ii. p. 431.

The words italicized (not by the author) are like thousands of similar instances in other writers and speakers ; but the sentence which follows the above deepens the impression by awaking a melancholy feeling: —

" Remembering the time when Clarkson began his career amid such opposition in Liverpool, we could not but regard such an evidence of its present public sentiment as full of encouragement."

We see no proportion nor contrast between this offer of a breakfast to our American antislavery friends and the original opposition to Clarkson.

Here is something entertaining : —

"A French gentleman who was greatly distressed in view of the sufferings of the negro race in America, said, naïvely enough, to Mrs. C——, that he had heard that the negroes had great capability for music, dancing, and the fine arts, and inquired whether something could not be done to move sympathy in their behalf, by training them to exhibit characteristic dances and pantomimes." — Vol. ii. p. 416.

Here I recalled the impressions made upon me by the respectable appearance and the religious demeanor of the slaves in southern towns and cities, and thought how little those slaves need this good monsieur to "move sympathy" for them, and what an injurious, insulting proposition this seems, to one recently from the south, that those slaves should be taken about to jump Jim Crow for the benefit of abolitionism. These "friends of the slaves," to whom this benighted speech was made, had no correction at hand for it; but

"Mrs. C—— quoted to him the action of one of the great ecclesiastical bodies in America, in the same breath declining to condemn slavery, but denouncing dancing as so wholly of the world lying in wickedness as to require condign ecclesiastical censure. The poor man was wholly lost in amazement." — Vol. ii. p. 416.

There is a strange comparison in this book of the French and American republics, in view of the abolition of slavery in French colonies, and our refusal to emancipate the slaves, who are a part of society here. Passing this, we come to the following, which is a great trial of American equanimity : —

"A deputation from Ireland here met me, presenting a

beautiful bog-oak casket, lined with gold, and carved with appropriate national symbols. They read a beautiful address, and touched upon the importance of inspiring with the principles of emancipation the Irish nation, whose influence in our land is becoming so great." — Vol. ii. p. 431.

To excite the poor Irish emigrants with zeal against American slavery is to some of equal importance with lifting them from their proximity to the brutes. One great cause of reluctance to emancipate, is and will continue to be, the fear that our colored people would become what these Irish are at home.

Once more. The writer is at the Pantheon in Paris.

" Now, this Pantheon seems to me a monument of the faults and the weakness of this very agreeable nation. Its history shows their enthusiasm, their hero worship, and the want of stabler religious convictions. Nowhere has there been such a want of reverence for the Creator, unless in the American Congress." — Vol. ii. p. 399.

There have been infidels, atheists, and all descriptions of men in the American Congress, individuals who have at times spoken in a way to pierce the heart of the country to the core. So in State legislatures, lyceums, conventions, freedom of speech has been indulged to licentiousness. But the American Congress maintain daily prayers and public worship on the Sabbath, and a private prayer meeting has for a long time been attended by a goodly number of that body. This comparison in the Pantheon of our national legislature with French infidels, in the matter of irreverence toward God, shows a state of feeling toward her country for which neither the writer's descent, education, or natural disposition is answerable, for they are above reproach ; but she is unduly affected by her party position with regard to slavery. She sees a negro standing in the sun, as she looks from foreign shores to her own land, and this is Uncle Tom's right ascension in her astronomy of our heavens. In her reperusal abroad of Walter Scott, did this writer forget the Lay of the Last Minstrel and never say to her soul —

"This is my own, my native land"?

Yes, but the book, the romance, had been written, and it created an atmosphere which is a sufficient apology for every thing. We enter an arrest of judgment for her against the poet. She shall not "forfeit fair renown." She will live, we trust, to change the tone of her present feelings, when the providence of God unfolds something more of his mysterious, but, we will persist in our hope, benevolent, purposes in connection with American slavery. When we all think and feel alike in regard to this perplexing and now inscrutable subject, we shall rejoice to see this prophetess in Africa's captivity taking her timbrel and leading us forth in songs and dances at Africa's redemption.

CHAPTER XIV.

BRITISH INTEREST IN AMERICAN SLAVERY.

THERE is no land in which the common people are better clothed, sheltered, and fed than in the United States, with the exception of one class; and that is, some who come to us from Great Britain, the poorer class of the Irish Catholics. Human nature in civilized life seldom goes down to worse degradation than in them, and the land that suffers such specimens of moral deformity to go from her, not in solitary instances, but in ship loads, never should offer compassionating prayers and exhortations, much less reproaches with regard to any other nation, until this class of her own subjects is improved. The most appropriate object in this country for British commiseration and tears, and for addresses from ladies to their sisters here, is the condition of their own people, exiles from Great Britain, some of whom look as the old Egyptians would on whom a few of the ten plagues should have made their mark. To go from their cellars and garrets in Boston and New York, and look upon the southern slaves enjoying not only the necessaries, but in towns and cities the luxuries, of life, indulged with all the comforts, and even, in many cases, with the superfluities, of dress, the most cheerful class of people that meets the eye of a stranger in this or any land, and every where enjoying the influences of pure religion, makes one consider what misplaced pity there is in British lamentations over American slavery.

The abolition of British slavery gives no right to speak to us even in the language of instruction. To abolish slavery in a foreign colony is like cutting off a wen from the body ; our slavery is in our constitution, our blood. Great Britain has never exercised any thing like the curative, painful, critical treatment which emancipation here would be to us. There is no parallel in raising twenty millions of pounds, and setting free the blacks of the British West Indies, to abolishing American slavery from the very warp and woof of human life in one third of this nation.

This venerable mother England, her hoary age reckoned by centuries, has only a few years since begun to reform certain dreadful oppressions and wrongs among her population at home, yet has seemed unwilling to allow her daughter, just come of age, a little time to dispose of one evil imposed upon us by her own hands, and which the country, as such, has no power to remove.

In Charlotte Elizabeth's Wrongs of Women, and Howitt's Rural Life in England, there are materials for a more powerful appeal to the feelings of humanity than can be found in American slavery, provided they could be wrought by true genius into the form of a tale. Indeed, there are appeals founded on facts, in the first-named book, in behalf of the milliners, seamstresses, pin makers, lace makers, and colliers of England, which leave an American reader at a loss to account for British interest, in years past, with regard to our slaves, while such disclosures and remonstrances were published in Great Britain. Well did Charlotte Elizabeth say, "Infanticide in India or China is a very awful thing;

slavery on the African coast makes our freeborn blood
tingle in our veins; and against both, man's lip can utter
most persuasive sounds of eloquent appeal, woman's
eye can shed a torrent of soft tears over the tale, but—
infanticide in Nottingham or Birmingham, slavery in
Manchester or Leeds — our excited feelings are calmed
down; the bright flame of our zeal expires." *

A good way to correct a morbid state of feeling pro-
duced by reading a novel founded on American slavery
is to read, for example, a piece by the above-named
writer, which parallels any thing which slavery has ever
furnished. Let it be remembered that the evils of slavery are mostly its abuses, but the evils depicted in
such descriptions as the one that follows are system-
atized wrongs, which within a few years the English
have begun to remove, but find that the abolition of evils
interwoven with society at home is not a simple and
easy work.

Nell Carter was employed about an English coal
mine, and Alice Smith, a villager's wife, had come
with her husband to the manufacturing district to
earn money. Nell unfolds to Alice the mysteries of
the pits : † —

"' You see that girl with red hair, the most foul-mouthed
young slut that ever used bad words; well, she is one of
nine children, all living in this place; and I think not one
of them knows who made 'em, they're so ignorant. Their
mother was a tidy girl, married, very young, to a miner;
and he had hardly got her into his power when he took her
down into the coal pits "to hurry" for him. You don't
know what that is? 'Tis the drawing of a wooden carriage, heavy loaded with coals, along the seams of a mine,

* Wrongs of Women, p. 278, New York ed.
† Ibid. pp. 99–101.

where a body couldn't stand half upright, where all is
dark as midnight, except the candlestick in the miner's
cap; and where she had to slave like a brute beast, in
nothing but her body linen, with a coarse pair of trousers,
a thick leathern belt round her waist, a heavy iron chain
fastened to it, passing between her legs and hooked on to the
carriage, and she dragging it, almost on all fours, through
these passages; ten, twelve, fourteen, or sixteen hours — I
was going to say every day — but there was no day for
her. It was dark night always in that frightful mine, and
dark nights above ground before she could leave it.

  " ' She toiled so for a few months, with her own husband to
drive her on in the work; but he found her earnings would
keep him idle half the week, and so he left her there — poor
young thing — among such a set that the worst you ever saw
here are angels to them. She worked till the morning of
the day her first child was born, — a lovely boy, — and had
to go down again in less than a fortnight, to the same life.
Till then, she had kept herself different from the rest; but
it seemed the parting her from the baby made her desperate. I was told her wild laugh would ring again through
the long, black galleries, and her jests keep them all merry;
but her heart was breaking as fast as it could then, and it
had broke. But we are blind creatures, and can't tell what
is best. It was a great lord owned all these mines; his
agent gave good wages, and got the worth of them out of
the miners too. Penrose, seeing the value his wife's toil
was of, took some pains to keep her from sinking, and she
came round a little, especially when he gave her a holiday
now and then to nurse her boy. She had that girl, yonder,
for her next; and by the time the third was born, I think
she'd as little of human nature left about her as could well
be found even in a coal pit. My heart has ached to see
her, all black and filthy, with a pipe in her mouth, swag-
gering or standing about, swearing and talking as nobody
in a Christian land should be let talk. And it was with her
own consent that at four years old her little boy was carried
down to his work in the pit.'

  " She pauses, for all the color has left Alice Smith's
face; then hastily resumes.

  " ' Don't suppose they set the baby "to hurry;" no, he
was only a trapper, sitting behind a door to pull it open
with a string, when any of the cobs came up. But it was
all in darkness, cold, and silence; and the child dared not
sleep through the long, long, black hours: and he said,
poor little thing! — but no matter for that; we will talk of

the mother. Ah, you begin to feel in your heart, now, that your lot isn't so bad as it might be! I see that. The poor woman bore ten or eleven children; nine lived, which was a wonder in all the place. She died at last by an awful death. One of her own children was winding at the pit's mouth, and, by carelessness natural in a child, overwound the rope; the bucket was drawn over the roller, and down, down she went, how many hundred feet I can not say; but there was no life in the mangled body.' "

While such fearful things as these abounded in the English collieries, and while every dressmaking establishment, as this writer says, in the language of an agent, "killed a gal a year," and Thomas Hood was writing the Song of the Shirt, addresses, remonstrances, were sent over by public bodies to this country, pleading for the slave. The ladies, who were responsible for the woes of the laboring classes of women, joined in appeals to their sisters here with regard to the condition of the slaves; but, most wonderful of all, remonstrances came from ecclesiastical bodies in Ireland, which was then depositing upon our shores a population which had few rivals in misery. Well may we use Whitefield's well-known exclamation, " Lord, what is man"! The truth is, this subject of slavery has been the occasion of more fanaticism than almost any thing since the crusades.

We will not recriminate; but a sense of injustice to us compels us to allude to one thing for which England has not exercised sufficient repentance, nor made sufficient atonement, to warrant many tears on our account. The wrongs and woes inflicted on young children in Great Britain have nothing to correspond with them in any Christian country. Allusion is made to this topic in the extract already given. There is a piece of poetry by Miss Barrett (Mrs. Browning) which is unsurpassed in the English language for its power to move the feelings,

called the " Cry of the Children." Sent down at four
years of age, many of them, to work under ground, they
find an eloquent pleader in this exquisite poetess, as
follows,(the dashes indicating imperfect quotations : —)

" Do ye hear the children weeping, O my brothers ? —
Do you question the young children in their sorrow ?
Your old earth, they say, is very dreary. —
Our young feet, they say, are very weak. —
The graves are for the old. —
Little Alice died last year ; —
We looked into the pit prepared to take her ;
There was no room for any work in the close clay ;
From the sleep wherein she lieth none will wake her,
Crying, Get up, little Alice ; it is day.
If you listen by that grave in sun and shower,
With your ear down, little Alice never cries. —
It is good when it happens, say the children,
That we die before our time. —
Go out, children, from the mine. —
Pluck the meadow cowslips. —
If we cared for any meadows, it were merely
To lie down in them and sleep. —
The reddest flowers would look as pale as snow."

" All day long the wheels are droning, turning ;
    Their wind comes in our faces ;
Till our hearts turn, and our heads with pulses burning,
    And the walls turn in their places.
Turns the sky in the high window, blank and reeling,
    Turns the long light that droopeth down the wall,
Turn the black flies, that crawl along the ceiling ;
    Are all turning all the day, and we with all ! —
And sometimes we could pray, —
O ye wheels, stop, be silent for a day." —

" And well may the children weep before ye ;
They are weary ere they run.
They know the grief of men, but not the wisdom ;
Are slaves without liberty in Christdom ;
Are martyrs by the pang without the palm."

Then comes this awful close : —

"How long, they say, how long, O cruel nation,
  Will you stand, to move the world, on a child's heart,
Trample down with mailed heel its palpitation,
  And tread onward to your throne amid the mart ?
Our blood splashes upward, O our tyrants,
  And your purple shows your path,
But the child's sob curseth deeper in the silence
  Than the strong man in his wrath."

A nation who had had such a piece as this written about
them, verified by commissioners of Parliament, ought
to have been sure that no trace of this enormous wrong
remained when they rejected American preachers for
not being up to their mark on the subject of abolishing
slavery, and before they remonstrated with slaveholders.
Let any one read Miss Barrett's piece at the south, in
sight of some little negroes, on any plantation, or in any
town or city. Their condition is paradise compared
with that of those whose " cry " is echoed by this lady.
What if the colored children in the slave States should
have had this piece read and explained to them, and an
address should have been written for them to Mrs.
Browning, thanking her for her interest in the suffering children of her own realm, and inviting her to
make the tour of the Southern States. We could have
made speeches and presented addresses about " the cry
of the children " in England which would have been
extremely distasteful across the water, especially if England itself were at that time exasperated by a sectional
controversy on the subject almost to the point of a civil
war.

It is an occasion for wonder to think of the common
antislavery feelings of our own people at the north, compared with the small amount of zeal and effort employed
in behalf of the British outcasts in our cities. Were such

meetings and such speeches as are employed to rouse up
the north against slavery used to direct public attention
to these unhappy creatures, no infidel orator at those
meetings would then be subjected to the divine reproach
of something worse, if possible, than his infidelity, name-
ly, of not providing for his own. When shall we send
food, and raiment, and shelter, and means of cleanliness,
not to say Christian teachers, to the poor of our own
cities, to the degree in which the slaves at the south enjoy these blessings? Let us use in behalf of our own
poor those stirring appeals drawn from "one blood," "all
men free and equal," " am I not a man and brother?"
and add, if we please, "Bunker Hill," " Bill of Rights,"
"American Independence." There are men, women,
and children, who are our neighbors, that need this eloquence in their behalf more than the slaves. They can
not recompense us, it is true, with notoriety; nor with
political advantage, except that we shall do most, in car-
ing for them, to save the country. You may establish
schools among these with no danger of imprisonment;
visit them in their miserable homes, and talk kindly to
them, without being suspected of incendiary motives;
protect fugitives from God and virtue without breaking
any laws. No chains about the Court House prevent you
from interposing as bail for tempted souls in their first
step into crime; no Mason's and Dixon's line makes a
boundary to your lawful zeal.   These poor ye have always with you, and when ye will ye may do them good.
If the saying be true, that a man who goes to law
should have clean hands, he who reproves others for neglect and sin should be sure that the God before whom he
arraigns them can not wither him by that rebuke, "Thou
hypocrite! first cast out the beam out of thine own eye!"

In the following extract from a late number of the New Orleans Creole, we see how the gospel is triumphing over well-known obstacles in that city : —

RELIGIOUS INSTRUCTION OF THE BLACKS IN NEW ORLEANS. — No one who has spent a month in New Orleans will deny the fact that the colored population of our city is a happy, well-dressed, and improving race. They are far above the poorer class, or day laborers, of northern towns, in all that tends to comfort and freedom from care.

It affords matter of astonishment, and an interesting subject for reflection, to those from the Northern States, to stand on the corners of any of our thoroughfares, of a Sabbath morning or an afternoon, and witness the constant succession of group after group of colored people, arrayed in plain, neat, and elegant attire, consisting often of whole families, from aged grandsire to toddling grandchild; their faces expressive of content and abundance; their conversation indicative of genuine happiness, as they wend their way to the various places of worship provided in the city for their accommodation. There is no countenance sharpened by want; there is no miserable caricature of humanity, redolent with filth, with rags fluttering in the breeze; there is no infantile visage crushed into the mould of age; but ever varied as our colored population is in features and dress, there is the undoubted proof of enjoyment, of plenty, of kind treatment, and of contentedness.

In the family circle, they receive religious instruction, as well as from the pulpits of their churches. The Sabbath school and the lecture room are open to their entrance.

We wandered, a week or two since, to the neighborhood of one of their principal places for worship. Before us the street was dotted with gay troops of black, brown, and tawny, on their way to the church. Long before we reached the edifice, the notes of sacred music broke upon the ear, chanted by voices of black worshipers. As we came to the door of the sacred edifice, a novel scene was presented. The pulpit was occupied by a preacher of ebony blackness; around the altar sat several white men, under whose especial care were the exercises of the occasion, who did not, however, interfere with the management of the religious services. There was a gravity in the gathered audience, filling the entire area of the building, which whiter congregations, in some places, might happily imitate.

It was soul-inspiring to witness the enthusiasm with which the hymn was sung, the whole audience rising in

token of respect; and untutored as were the voices of the
many, a note of liquid sweetness was heard, which would
have brought down the theatrical critics with thunders of
applause. When the prayer was offered, they all bowed,
as though each one was personally interested in the petition, fervently but rudely uttered. How simply the wants
of that crowd were presented! How trustingly the petition was made!

The topic of the preacher was the glory of heaven.
The speaker knew his hearers. He adapted his language
to their capacity. We can not avoid giving an instance of
illustration, apt and forcible : —

" My bredren," said he, as he pointed to a stagnant ca-
nal and filthy thoroughfare, " de streets here am full ob
mud; de water still until it is full of corruption ; de hot sun
makes it steam up with bad smells, and often fill de whole
city wid death.   But, bressed be God, my bredren, dare is
no muddy streets in heben : dare are golden pavements
and pure waters, and de air is full ob de smell ob de violet
and de rose, and de face ob God ever makes de place glo-
rious wid hebenly light."

The muttered exclamation of assent showed he had
awakened the feelings of his hearers ; and the swinging
to and fro of the crowds proved the enthusiasm with which
they were moved.

This scene is repeated on a smaller or larger scale all
over the south.   The Methodist and Baptist black churches
in this city have a very large number of communicants.
It is generally acknowledged, by all classes of the community, that religious advantages for the slave are imper-
atively demanded from the master.

Our plantation slaves on the coast have their regular
ministers in religious things ; generally a white clergyman
of standing, who preaches at three or four places of a Sabbath day.

We are familiar with the means of religious instruction
for the poor in northern cities, and we can safely aver that
their advantages fall far short of those granted the blacks
of the south.

CHAPTER XV.

THE BIBLE AND SLAVERY.

WHEN the Hebrew nation was organized oy the Most
High, he found among the people masters and slaves.
He could have purged out slaveholding by positive
enactments; he could have rid the people of all the
slave owners by making their dead bodies fall in the wilderness. Instead of this, he made slavery the subject
of legislation, prescribed its duties, and protected the
parties concerned in the performance of them.

But who can withhold his tribute of love and adoration at the divine goodness and wisdom which mark the
whole Mosaic code, as illustrated in that honorable regard for man, as man, which strove continually to lift and
break the yoke of bondage to his fellow-man from his
neck? They who assert that the Bible sanctions the
relation of master and slave are bound to show in what
spirit and with what intentions the Most High permitted the relation to remain. Otherwise they commit
the fearful mistake of making infinite goodness and wisdom countenance oppression.

There are some extremely interesting and even beautiful illustrations in the Bible of the destiny of involuntary servitude to be from the first a waning, transient
relation. Every thing pointed to freedom as the desirable condition; easements, deliverances from it, were

skillfully prepared in the Hebrew constitution. Maiming, concubinage, the children of concubines, years of release, jubilees, all the various conditions and seasons connected with the termination of bondage, show that slavery was a condition out of which it is the destiny of human nature to rise; and falling into it is a calamity, a retrogression.

The preferableness of freedom to slavery, in the divine mind and plan, is set forth in the passage where Jeremiah, in the name of God, directed, in the last days of the nation, that every Hebrew servant should be manumitted according to law; for afflictions were making them break off their sins. This divine injunction was obeyed; but afterwards they reconsidered their repentance, and the servants were reduced again to bondage. God appeals to them against this outrage, by reminding them of Egypt, and of his appointment in their early history of years of release, and charges them with "polluting" his name by the reëstablishment of slavery over those who had a right to liberty, threatening them for this in these words of awful irony: "Behold, I proclaim a liberty for you, saith the Lord, to the sword, to the pestilence, and to the famine; and I will make you to be removed into all the kingdoms of the earth." *

The New Testament speaks out, not in ordinances, but in words, and teaches more distinctly that freedom is to be preferred when it may be had. "If thou mayest be free, use it rather."

It is as though bondage were incident to darkness and twilight, and removable only by the clear sunlight of a state of society which would be incompatible with every

* Jer. xxxiv. 8–22.

form of oppression. So we find that wherever the influence of religion reaches a high point, slavery wholly
changes its character, though it may continue in form and
name. It may be benevolent to individuals, to a class,
that the form of slavery remain; but in such a case the
yoke is broken, and to fight against the form and the
name, when the thing itself had ceased to be an evil,
would be to fight a shadow.

The wise manner in which the Apostles deal with
slavery is one incidental proof of their inspiration.
The hand of the same God who framed the Mosaic code
is evidently still at work in directing his servants, the
Apostles, how to deal with slavery. Men with their
benevolence and zeal, if left to themselves, would, some
of them, have gone to extremes on that subject; for
" ultraism," as we call it, is the natural tendency of good
men, not fully instructed, in their early zeal. The disposition to put away a heathen husband or wife, abstain-
ing from marriage and from meats, Timothy's omission
to take wine in sickness, show this, and make it remarkable that slavery was dealt with as it was by the
Apostles. Only they who had the Spirit of God in them
could have spoken so wisely, so temperately, with regard
to an evil which met them every where with its bad
influences and grievous sorrows. Some in their day, who
professed to be Christian teachers, were " ultraists," and
could not restrain themselves, but evidently encouraged
servants not to count their masters worthy of all honor,
and to use the equality of divine grace to them and their
believing masters, as a claim to equality in other things,
thus despising their believing masters because they were
brethren. Never is the Apostle Paul more severe in the
use of epithets than in denouncing such teachers and

their doctrines. Far as possible from countenancing servitude as a condition which man has a right to perpetuate, or to which any class of men is doomed, but declaring plainly that freedom is to be preferred by the slave, he and his fellow-laborers employed themselves in disseminating those principles and that spirit which would make slavery as an oppression impossible, changing its whole nature by abolishing all the motives which create such an institution. But as it is not sunrise in every place at the same moment, and in places where the sun has risen there are ravines and vales, where the light is slow to enter, so we can not expect that the evils of slavery will disappear at once, even where the religion of Christ generally prevails; but in proportion as it extends its influence, slavery is sure to cease in all its objectionable features. An interesting illustration of this, on a large scale, is afforded by the state of slavery in the United States and Cuba. Spanish slavery has a very mild code, but is severe and oppressive. American slavery has perhaps as rigid a code as any; but practically, it is the mildest form of involuntary servitude, and few would justify themselves in doing no better for their slaves than the law requires. Pure religion must have the credit of this difference, teaching us that to remove slavery we must promote spiritual religion, and to this end use every means to propagate Christian knowledge and Christian charity.

We are not as wise as Paul if we withdraw our Christian teachers and books, imbued with the great principles of pure religion, from communities where we are not allowed to do all the good which we may desire, or to present a duty in such specific forms as our preferences dictate. Our principle ought not to be, to abandon men as soon as we are resisted, or can not say and do all that we would ; but we should study ways to remain, trusting to the power of light and love to open doors for us. The dust which we too readily shake off from our feet against men will be a witness against us, rather than against them. It must gratify the arch enemy to see us withdraw our forces in solemn indignation at his show of resistance. The children of this world do not suffer themselves to be so easily foiled, nor do they force unacceptable offerings upon Japan, but ply her with things to tempt her desire for further commodities, representing their usefulness in ways which do not excite national jealousy and pride.

It is refreshing to escape from those books of overheated zeal which attack slavery, and read the passages in the New Testament relating to the subject ; breathing a spirit fatal to oppression, yet counseling no measures against it because of its seeming trust in its own omnipotent influence wherever it shall build its throne.

Paul's refusal to interfere between Onesimus and his master is one of those gentle lessons of wisdom on this subject which are so characteristic of his spirit in dealing with this public evil. That small epistle to Philemon, that one chapter, that little piece of parchment, that mere note of apology, — that this should have fallen into the sacred canon, and not the epistle to Laodicea, is curious and interesting to those who regard the providence of God in the canon of Scripture. That little writing is like a small, firm beach, where storms have beaten, but have left it pure and white. It is the least of all seeds in Paul's Epistles. It is a curiosity of inspiration, a solitary idiom in a language, a Stonehenge in a country, a warm stream in the sea ; it begins with loving salutations, ends with affectionate Christian messages, and sends back a servant to his master and to a system of slavery under which this fugitive could, if his master required, be put to death. Now, he who argues from this that he has an unqualified right to reclaim his slave, and subject him to just such treatment as he pleases, is as much at fault as those who are at the other extreme. It was to a Philemon that Onesimus was returned ; it was to Abraham's house that Hagar was remanded. While the abstract principle of ownership is defended by these examples, he who uses them to the injury of a fellow-being will find that God has stores of vengeance for him, and that his own "Master in heaven" is the inexorable Judge.

The difference in the Apostles' way of dealing with slavery, and with other evils, teaches clearly that the relation itself is not in their view sinful. Many insist that it is sinful, that the Apostles must so have regarded it, and that the reason why they did not attack it is, they would not interfere with the laws and government. It is said " they girdled slavery, and left it to die."

But this surely is not in accordance with the apostolic spirit. There is no public wickedness which they merely girdled and left to die. Paul did not quietly pass his axe round the public sins of his day. His divine Master did not so deal with adultery and divorces. James did not girdle wars and fightings, governmental measures. Let Jude be questioned on this point, with that thunderbolt of an Epistle in his hand. Even the beloved disciple disdained this gentle method of dealing with public sins when he prophesied against all the governments of the earth at once.

But slavery, declared by some to be the greatest sin

against God's image in man, most fruitful, it is said, of evils, is not assaulted, but the sins and abuses under it are reproved, the duties pertaining to the relation of master and slave are prescribed, a slave is sent back to servitude with an inspired epistle in his hand, and slavery itself is nowhere assailed. On the contrary, masters are instructed and exhorted with regard to their duties as slaveholders. Suppose the instructions which are addressed to slaveholders to be addressed to those sinners with whom slaveholders are promiscuously classed by many, for example : " Thieves, render to those from whom you may continue to steal, that which is just and equal." "And, ye murderers, do the same things unto your victims, forbearing threatening." " Let as many as are cheated count their extortioners worthy of all honor." If to be a slave owner is in itself parallel with stealing and other crimes, miserable subterfuge to say that Paul did not denounce it because it was connected with the institutions of society; that he " girdled it, and left it to die." Happy they whose principles with regard to slavery enable them to have a higher opinion of Paul than thus to make him a timeserver and a slave to expediency.

But was he therefore " a proslavery man " ? Not he. Would he have spoken against the system of American slavery had he lived in our day ? Surely he would ; against its evils, its abuses, its sins, but not against the relation of master and slave. Suppose that Philemon had thrown Onesimus into prison for absconding, and Paul had heard of his having lain there three months till he was sick with jail fever, and likely to die. If he could have reached Philemon through church discipline, and the offender had persisted in his sin, we can imagine Paul directing the church "in the name of the Lord Jesus to deliver such an one to Satan for the destruction of the flesh, that the spirit may be saved in the day of the Lord Jesus." Any church that suffers a member to deal wrongfully with his servant, or suffers a slave member to be recklessly sold, has in Paul's epistles single words and whole sentences which ought to make it quail. Yet there is not a word there against the relation of master and slave; and for what reason?

The way in which the Apostles evidently purposed to remove slavery, was by creating a state of things in which it would cease. This method is not analogous to girdling trees, but to another process resorted to by husbandmen. Their only method of expelling certain weeds — sorrel, for example — is, to enrich the soil. The gospel is to slavery what the growing of clover is to sorrel. Religion in the masters destroys every thing in slavery which makes it obnoxious; and not only so, it converts the relation of the slave into an effectual means of happiness. In many instances at the south, for example, slavery is no more slavery so long as those masters live; and if religion were every where predominant, their servants would not suffer by the death of their masters any more than by time and chance, which happen to all. Religion will never remove men's need of being served and of serving; but it will make service an honorable and happy employment, under whatever name it may pass. And as farmers do not attack weeds for the mere sake of expelling them, but to use their place for something better, so the New Testament does not attack slavery to drive it out, but gets possession of the heart, which is naturally tyrannical and covetous, and, filling it with the fruits of the Spirit, the works of the flesh disappear.

When a man repents and is converted, he does not repent of his sins one by one, but there is a state of heart created within him, with regard to all sin, which constitutes repentance. In accordance with this we do not find the Bible laboring merely to make a man specifically penitent, but it uses one sin and another to lead the man back to that heart which is the root of all his sins. Those who preach to convicts tell us that when they are convinced of sin, if they fix their thoughts upon particular transgressions, and make them the special subjects of repentance, one of two things happens; they either see the whole of their sin and misery by means of these instances of wickedness, or they confine their thoughts to these items, and then become superficial and self-righteous. David's sin, as we see by the fifty-first Psalm, led him to feel and deplore his ruined nature. Many attempts to reform particular evils in society which grow out of human wickedness have no effect to make men true penitents, though reformations of morals and of abuses are always auxiliary to religion; but if an equal amount of zeal employed in assailing abuses were employed in promoting Christian piety and charity by diffusing Christian knowledge and ordinances, and also by the influence of a good temper and spirit, especially where Christian men are the objects of our zeal, and their coöperation and influence are our surest means of success, we should see changes in society brought about in a healthful way, which would be permanent because of the basis of character on which they would rest. But all this antifebrile sentiment is scorned by overheated zealots. Still there is sound discretion in these words of Dr. Chalmers: —

"I have been a projector in my day, and, much as I have been employed with the economics of society, my conviction is more and more strengthened in the utter vanity of all expedients short of faith in the gospel of Jesus Christ; whose disciples are the salt of the earth, and through whose *spirituality and religion, alone,* we can look for the permanent civilization and comfort of the species, or even for earthly blessings; which come after, and not before, the kingdom of God and his righteousness." *

The apostolic spirit with regard to slavery, surely, is not of the same tone with the spirit which encourages slaves every where to flee from their masters, and teaches them that his swiftest horse, his boat, his purse, are theirs, if they wish to escape. Philemon, traveling with Onesimus, was not annoyed by a vigilance committee of Paul's Christian friends with a habeas corpus to rescue the servant from his master; nor did these friends watch the arrival of ships to receive a fugitive consigned by " the saints and faithful brethren which were at Colossé" to the "friends of the slave" at Corinth. True, these disciples had not enjoyed the light which the Declaration of American Independence sheds on the subject of human rights. Moses, Paul, and Christ were their authorities on moral subjects; but our infidels tell us that we should have a far different New Testament could it be written for us now; but since we can not have a new Bible now and then, this proves that " God can not make a revelation to us in a book." Every man, they say, must decide as to his duty by the light of present circumstances, not by a book written eighteen hundred years ago. Zeal against American slavery has thus been one of the chief modern foes to the Bible. Let him who would not become an infidel and atheist beware and not follow his sensibilities, as affected by cases of distress, in preference

* Sab. Readings, Deut. xxxiv.

to the word of God, which the unhappy fate of some who have made shipwreck of their faith in their zeal against slavery shows to be the best guide.

I may be allowed to state the manner in which my own mind was relieved at the south with regard to the prospects of slavery. From youth, I had believed that its removal is essential to our continued existence as a nation, and yet no one saw in what way this change was to be effected. My error was in supposing that the blacks must be removed in order to remove slavery, or, that they must be emancipated; that we must have some "first of August" to mark a general manumission. Now there are many slaveholders at the south who make the condition of their slaves as comfortable and happy as the condition of the same persons could be in any circumstances. Wicked men are permitted by the present laws to practise iniquity and oppression; but when the influence of good men so far prevails as to make laws which will restrain and govern those who are susceptible to no influence but that of authority, the form of slavery will be all pertaining to it which will remain, and this only while it is for the highest good of all concerned, and acknowledged to be so by both parties, the doom of the blacks, as a race, being abandoned, and the interests of each individual, his inclination and aptitude, being regarded in finding employment for him. I saw that if good men at the south were left to themselves without annoyance by foreign intervention, the spirit of the New Testament with regard to slavery might ere long be fulfilled. Nor would the Old Testament jubilee, or seventh year release, be necessary; these, like other things in Moses, being done away in Christ by the bestowal of liberty, or protection under Christian masters; no ceremonial, therefore, being needed to effect or announce their liberty, and jubilees and seventh years, indeed, not coming fast enough, and being too formal for the times. Let us feel and act fraternally with regard to the south, defend them against interference, abstain from every thing assuming and dictatorial, leave them to manage their institution in view of their accountability to God, and, if we please, in view of the line upon line and precept upon precept which we, their many and very capable instructors, male and female, have vouchsafed to them, and we may expect that American slavery will cease to be any thing but a means of good to the African race. When no longer available for good, the form itself will be abolished.

Suppose that we should receive a report from missionaries giving an account of three millions of people brought out of heathenism and elevated to the position of the slaves in our Southern States. While we should join with the missionaries to deplore remaining evils and certain liabilities to evil among them, we should fill our prayers with praises at the marvelous work of grace among that people. And were the foreign lords of that people generally in favor of their improvement, and very many of them examples of all kindness and faithfulness, we should be careful how we interfered with the leaven which was leavening, slowly, but surely, the whole mass of the population. Some, however, as now, would wish to precipitate the process.

In addition to what has been said of the way in which the gospel will affect slavery, it may be observed that common humanity, self-interest, and law may, each in its own method, do all the good in its power, without waiting for the higher motives of spiritual religion.

Nor are we to neglect or disparage means and measures which tend to good, though actuated merely by considerations of policy. Yet spiritual religion is God's chosen instrument of doing the greatest amount of good in the best possible way. It puts every thing at work for its object; it purifies our motives; it makes the result permanent; it saves men from the temptations incident to victory and defeat.

CHAPTER XVI.

FEELINGS OF SLAVES, AND FEELINGS FOR THE SLAVES, CONTRASTED.

THE feelings and language of some leading opposers of slavery are greatly to be deplored for the bad effect which they have upon the country and upon the best interests of the slave. No one can be at the south for a while and not feel that the spirit, language, and measures of such men are very hurtful, being not only useless, but positively frustrating the good which is professedly sought.

At the south, after reading the report of an abolition meeting in New York in May last, at which the speakers seemed to be in throes of anguish on account of slavery, and were for dissolving the Union, declaring also the Christian church to be the great defender of the greatest of sins, and representing the house of bondage at the south as a universal mass of corruption through festering sins and wounds, I happened to attend a religious meeting of slaves on the Sabbath. Their pastor, a white man, preached a sermon to them on the assurance of Christian hope. They stood up to sing. Such was the evident contrast between the report of the meeting in New York, with its infidelity and almost blasphemy, and this company of worshiping slaves, that it seemed to me, could that song of the slaves have broken in upon the abolition meeting, it would have been to it almost as when one in another place " saw

Abraham afar off and Lazarus in his bosom." The
pastor from the pulpit called on one of the colored men
to conclude with prayer. He kneeled before a seat in
the aisle, an elderly negro with a gray head, and seemed
to forget that there was any ear but that of God that
listened to his humble, earnest prayer. Thus, while
some are burning the Constitution and pulling down the
fabric of the American Union to rid themselves of slavery, the great plan of human redemption, as it respects
the African race, is proceeding noiselessly at the south,
and there is joy more frequently perhaps in the presence of the angels of God over a penitent sinner there
than among the same number of souls in any part of
our land. One of the best of men, who ministers to a
church having on its list twenty-seven hundred blacks,
writes to me, " In the church I serve there are some
of the most beautiful specimens of Christian character
I ever saw. Often have I witnessed the calm, intelligent, triumphant death bed, and have said in my soul, I
shall not be fit to sit at the feet of these in heaven. I
experience from them great affection, and regret most
deeply that, as reputation among men can not operate as
an incentive to preparation, I have not a more simple
love to Christ and souls to urge me to diligence in
studying for the pulpit."

A slave, with a subdued, touching face, stood up one
evening in a prayer meeting of the colored people, and
broke the silence by repeating two lines at a time of the
hymn beginning thus : —

> " How sad our state by nature is !
>   Our sin how deep it stains !
> And Satan binds our captive minds
>   Fast in his slavish chains.

> " But there's a voice of sovereign grace," &c.

It would seem strange to many that a slave should feel that there are "chains" more to be deplored than those of southern slavery; but they would find in the religious meetings of the colored people that there is a bondage which, in the view of the slaves, would more appropriately be the subject of certain conventions which have been held, than American slavery — a bondage which makes infidel opposers of slavery proper objects of compassion and subjects of prayer with the slaves as they look down with concern from their religious assemblies upon those unbelievers who meet to pity them.

Tens of thousands among them feel and speak as one of them did to whom in conversation I ventured to put the question whether he would like to be free. Twisting the withes of old grape vines around the ends of rails in mending a fence, he thought a moment, turned his face toward me, while he held a rail, half tied, in its place, and emphasizing his words with motions of his head, he replied, each word being deliberately separated from the rest: "I want to be free from my sins; them's all my burden; and if I can get that, the balance of the rest may go from me." We were in the woods alone; I had spoken of heaven; he feared he should "never see that happy place;" I spoke of pardon through Christ; his hopes revived; he promised that he would look to Christ alone for salvation, and after I had gone from him some way, he broke out with the well-known tune of Ortonville: —

> "Majestic sweetness sits enthroned
> Upon the Saviour's brow."

The woods were filled with his powerful voice. I thought of those words, which can seldom be quoted at

the present day with safety to one's reputation as being
" right on the subject of slavery," but which were illustrated in him — " Art thou. called being a servant ?
care not for it." Paul evidently was not so much distressed in his mind about slavery and the slaves, as
some of us are who know less about slavery than he,
and feel far less than he what it is to be " called."

We frequently hear it said, referring to the duty of removing slavery, that we must break every yoke. Many
who say this reckon that in the United States there are
three million two hundred and four thousand three hundred and thirteen " yokes," this being the number of
slaves.

Now, you can not pass through the south and not see
that a very large number may at once be struck from
this reckoning of yokes ; that there are very many slaves
who, if you should propose to break a " yoke " for them,
would not understand you. The question is not as to
enslaving a new people ; nor does it relate to the An-
tilles, nor to Guiana, nor to Mexico ; it relates to these
people who are here ; and the proper question is not an
abstract one with regard to slavery, but what is best for
this people in their circumstances. The troubles which
we impute to their condition are many of them like the
most of our own, viz., " borrowed troubles ; " we make
them in our thoughts bear the burdens of all the possible evils which theoretically belong to the system of
slavery. Even if we take all these into view, the amount
of happiness among them compares favorably with that
among the same number of people elsewhere. If there
are some evils to which they are exposed, there are
others from which they are exempt. The feeling involuntarily arose within me at the south, and especially

in the religious meetings of the slaves, Would that all Africa were here! Could villages and tribes of Africans be by any means induced to emigrate to this land, and be placed under the influences which the slaves enjoy, Ethiopia would stretch out her hands to God sooner than the most sanguine interpreters of prophecy now dare to hope. It is deeply affecting to hear the slaves give thanks in their prayers that they have not been left like the heathen who know not God, but are raised, as it were, to heaven in their Christian privileges.

CHAPTER XVII.

CHEERFUL VIEWS. — CONCLUSION.

WE ought to be the happiest people on earth. The strongest mutual affection should exist between the different parts of a country constituted as we are. Our family of States, so many sovereignties governing themselves, yet consenting to be governed, like constellations, each with its own order and laws, but all obeying one great rule, suggesting, as organized communities, more than any other nation, the divine pattern of the tribes in the Hebrew commonwealth; our heroic origin surpassing even the fabulous romantic beginnings of other nations, but superior to them in its pious and benevolent motives; the names of our States holding charmed associations of adventure and exploit, the Indian relics, shrined in the names, growing more and more interesting with age; our enthusiastic union in times of peril; the reception, one by one, of new members into the household, and thereupon one star after another quietly taking its place in the field of our flag; the beautiful respect paid to the humblest member of the family by her equality of representation in the Senate with the proudest State; our territory compassed overhead by such a zone and around by oceans, yet the sea shores exceeded by the coasts of navigable inland lakes; our rivers; our soil adapted to almost every culture; the absence of social disabilities, and the political equality of the citizens; our freedom of faith and speech; our rulers chosen by the people; our ability to receive and protect the oppressed of other lands; our schools, our Sabbath, our vigorous manhood, reached at the period of the world's history when we can be preëminently useful by our example and influence, — bring together more elements of happiness for a nation than are elsewhere found.

It might well be said to us, "Beloved, if God so loved us, we ought also to love one another."

The providence of God, as it shall unfold with regard to the African race, will no doubt greatly affect our hearts. We are apprehending trouble and sorrow on account of this people. In the abyss of the future we hear such confused noises as might have been heard in the sounding deep of chaos, when mountains and seas were jostling into their places. Order was asserting her sway, and at the present time, while "chains and slavery" fill the ears and appall the hearts of many, some great development of providence with regard to the African race may be approaching. Let us settle this in our minds, that progress and improvement are to be the rule of human destiny, and let us have patience one with another. Never, we are constrained to think, could slavery have existed so long amidst such influences of Christianity as prevail in this country, and such efforts of the southern people themselves to abolish it, were it not that God intends to use us as the chief instruments of good to the African race. Therefore he has suffered us to be greatly afflicted on account of them; and now he may be leading us to the brink of ruin by our connection with this people, to show us that we must unite to redeem and bless them, if it be only for our own preservation. Their increase has averaged in each ten years four or five per centum more than that of the whites. Had it not been for the foreign immigration of white persons, they would have been in 1850 nearer to an equality with the whites by three hundred and fifty or four hundred, thousand. The time must come when the slaves will outnumber the whites in some districts of the country. A leader only will be necessary to place them in a position in which they can make their own terms with us. Surely we are bound by sentiments of common human brotherhood, not to say by ties of country, to look upon the south not as an enemy, but as one whom we would invite and encourage to lead our efforts in union with theirs in behalf of this people.*

We turn to our southern brethren and friends, therefore, and with no obtrusive zeal we beg them to let us stand related to them, and to this subject, as their friends and brethren; not repelling us, but encouraging every sign of desire to promote a good understanding. Let us together wait and hope till Providence discloses ways of doing good to the African race, in which we shall have been prepared to coöperate by a previous cultivation of mutual good feelings. God will not leave us always to contend together. "The north and the south, thou hast created them; Tabor and Hermon shall rejoice in thy name."

A young missionary from the south was embarking for Africa. His mother was taking leave of him; her

* See some valuable statistics with regard to the blacks in this country, in several articles in the Boston Courier, ending March 2, 1853, understood to be from the pen of Dr. J. Chickering.

arms were round his neck. She cried, "O Granville, Granville, my dear son, how can I give you up!" The son, without embracing his mother, stood, and lifted his arms above her, and stretched them out beyond her, and cried, louder than his mother, "O Africa, Africa, how can I give you up!" At foreign missionary meetings in the Southern States I noticed that African missions interested the people most deeply. The south is best qualified to lead the whole country in plans and efforts for the African race. We will follow her.

In the first part of this book I have spoken of a choir whose performances were not so cultivated as edifying; but there was one occasion, when, in listening to the performances of a colored choir on the Sabbath, it is no exaggeration to say that I enjoyed more than in the performance of sacred music at any time by any other choir, such was the perfect time, accentuation, judicious stress, varied movement, and just conception of the sentiments of the hymns sung by fifteen voices of remarkable variety. One development of African talent hereafter will no doubt be in music. Even now we have illustrations of the power which some of their popular airs have over the common mind in whistling boys, and military bands, and the merry making parlor music. The colored people will give us music of a natural order, full of genuine feeling, opening its way directly to the general heart. Their voices probably surpass all voices known to us in sweetness, compass, and power; male tenor voices, so rare among us, abound among them ; large additions to human happiness await us from this source, under proper cultivation. In the choir now alluded to there was a man whose voice was like a reed instrument; and in other choirs and meetings no such vocal phenomena have ever occurred to me as among the blacks. This choir sung a hymn, a voluntary performance, at the opening of public worship, which in the state of mind with which I was thinking of the slaves, seemed as though I was hearing it sung to them by those who sung over Bethlehem at the nativity. That slaves, — though a few of this choir were free, — that these representatives of Africa, should sing this hymn with perfect skill and deep feeling, seemed beautifully prophetic. The tune was "Marton," in Cantica Laudis:

> "On the mountain top appearing,
>   Lo, the sacred herald stands,
> Joyful news to Zion bearing,
>   Zion long in captive lands.
>   Mourning captive!
>   God himself will loose thy bands.
>
> "Lo, thy sun is risen in glory;
>   God himself appears thy friend;
> All thy foes shall flee before thee;
>   Here their boasted triumphs end.
>   Great deliverance!
>   Zion's King vouchsafes to send.
>
> "Enemies no more shall trouble;
>   All thy wrongs shall be redressed;
> For thy shame thou shalt have double,
>   In thy Maker's favor blest.
>   All thy conflicts
>   End in an eternal rest."

Those who wait for the consolation of Africa, and who love to sing, can make this hymn and tune keep fresh their best affections for that people, and help their petitions for the approach of the time when "for their shame they shall have double, and for confusion they shall rejoice in their portion."

If the nations of the earth celebrate in heaven their national experiences under the providence and grace of God, Africa's song will probably do as much as any to illustrate them. But who will write Africa's hymn? What mysteries of providence and grace, what remembrances of woe, what corresponding heights of joy and bliss, what forgiveness and love, what adoration, what sweet affections born of chastisement, what appreciation of heaven, with its liberty, and equality, and recompense of patient suffering, will that hymn contain, and with what voices will it be sung! No man can learn that song, no man can write it, but some African slave. We from America shall listen to that song with feelings unlike those of any other nation.

If there were truth in the fancy that angels are permitted to invent flowers, he must have been the most original, and the most to be wondered at, who invented the cactus, the rough, misshapen thing, which puts forth a flower surpassed by nothing in the kingdom of nature. As though to vex and repel for a time, and then to astonish, and to secure the love and care of woman; as though it were a hieroglyphic, coarse in its engraving and exquisite in its sense; an emblem of God's afflictions and their fruits in those whom he loves; a promise vegetating; faith, having no sight; hope, with the reward of patience concealed in it, — this cactus always impressed me more than any other plant. When, at the south, I spent a morning in a burying ground of the colored people, reading the simple, touching inscriptions, —

" Their names, their years, spelt by the unlettered muse," —

and saw, all about in the grass, the prickly pear, embryo cactuses, gathering round the graves of the slaves, I felt no need of one to interpret for me.   The deep murmur in the tops of the pines overhead, with the birds singing in the branches, comported well with the discovery of this token of present, thorny sorrow, this emblem of Africa in her past history and her coming beauty, and in the love which she is to win from all hearts.

THE END.